REAL
❧ COOKERY ❧

a 21 Day
Course

REAL INDIAN COOKERY

❧ **COOKERY** ☙

a 21 Day Course

Veena Chopra

foulsham

LONDON • NEW YORK • TORONTO • SYDNEY

foulsham

The Publishing House, Bennetts Close,
Cippenham, Berkshire SL1 5AP

ISBN 0 572 01958 0

Copyright © 1994 Veena Chopra

Printed in: Cox & Wyman Ltd., Reading, Berkshire.

Dedication

I dedicate this book to:
Papa and Biji - My parents
Pritam - My husband
Sumeet - My son
Sajni - My daughter

About The Author

Veena Chopra was born in the Punjab and grew up in a large household with many relations living together and several servants. Educated in Uttar Pradesh, she was an enthusiastic cook from childhood. In 1959 she received 1st prize for cooking in the Shajhanpur district. She trained as a teacher and is a post graduate of Agra University India.

She was married in 1970, after seeing her husband for only half an hour a few days before the wedding – as the marriage was arranged by her parents. She came to England with her husband who is a physics teacher, four days after the marriage. They now live in Cambridge and have two children called Sumeet and Sajni.

Veena is a science co-ordinator at Blue Gate Fields Junior School and also teaches Indian Cookery at many Cambridgeshire Community Colleges during the evening, she has given cookery demonstrations on Saturdays and has also been invited to do cookery demonstrations at various Women Institute Centres.

Veena sometimes gives demonstrations, with her two children, of traditional Indian dances at local Cultural Exhibitions and at various places in London. She enjoys playing the sitar.

This is Veena's second Indian cookery book. She is currently working on her third manuscript.

Indian Cookery in 21 Days

Introduction   11/12
A few points to remember   13/16
Miscellaneous   18/27

Day 1
Egg curry   30
Puri (Bread)   32
Coconut and Chocolate Barfi (Sweet)   34

Day 2
Sindhi Style Meat   38
Chapati (Bread)   40
Tomato, Cucumber & Onion Rayta (Yoghurt)   41

Day 3
Vegetable Samosa   44
Tamarind Chutney   48
Jalebi (Sweet)   50

Day 4
Prawn Pulao   54
Khatéwalé Kabuli Chunna (Chickpeas)   56
Bhutoora (Bread)   58

Day 5
Stuffed Murgh Musallum (chicken dish)   62
Roghni Nan (Bread)   66
Lassi (Drink)   68

Indian Cookery in 21 Days

Day 6
Stuffed Bread Rolls   72
Gulab Jamun (Sweet)   74
Dhaniya Chutney (Coriander)   76

Day 7
Pork or Lamb Vindaloo   80
Green Whole Moong (Lentil)   82
Kulfi (Indian Ice-cream)   84
Falooda   85

Day 8
Dosa (Bread)   88
Coconut Chutney   90
Fried Fish   92
Vegetable Pulao (Rice)   94

Day 9
Pakora (Onion Bhaji)   98
Dalmod (Bombay Mix)   100

Day 10
Onion Paratha (Bread)   108
Aloo, Gobhi and Gosht (Potato, Cauliflower
   and Lamb)   110
Mixed Vegetable Korma   112
Urud Ki Sukhi Dal (Lentil)   114

Indian Cookery in 21 Days

Day 11
Matar Paneer (Peas and Indian Cheese)   118
Chicken Mughlai Biryani   120
Tirangi Barfi (Sweet)   123

Day 12
Sweet and Sour Prawns   128
Aloo Paratha (Bread)   132
Dhandai (Drink)   134

Day 13
Chicken Curry   138
Whole Cauliflower   140
Carrot Halwa (Sweet)   143

Day 14
Rogan Josh (Lamb dish)   146
Sambar (Lentil)   148
Idli (Bread)   150

Day 15
Dhansank   154
Fried Bhindi or Okra (Ladyfinger)   157
Sabudana Papar   158

Day 16
Aloo Ki Tikiya (Potato Cutlets)   162
Gol Guppa   164

Indian Cookery in 21 Days

Papri 166
Fruit Chát 168

Day 17
Creamed Chicken 172
Chola Dal (Lentil) 174
Bharta (Aubergine) 176

Day 18
Keema Kabab 180
Aloo Katchori (Bread) 182
Stuffed Green Pepper 184

Day 19
Chicken Tikka 190
Gajar Matar Ki Sabji (Carrot and Peas Curry) 192
Gujiya (Sweet) 194

Day 20
Puri Walé Aloo (Potato Curry) 198
Rajma (Red-beans) 200
Fish Curry 202

Day 21
Dry Meat Masala 208
Stuffed Tomato 210
Rasgulla (Sweet) 212
Vegetable Biryani (Rice) 214

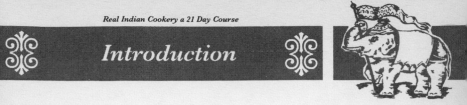

Introduction

This book has been written for all those who enjoy Indian food. Every part of India is different, its people and customs varied. Each area prides itself with a particularly special cuisine. Emigrant Indians have kept the flag of their native food's fragrance and the flavour is flying all over the world.

No one is a born cook. Practice, curiosity and need makes one perfect. For instance, my mother had never cooked before her marriage. The first day after her wedding she was asked by Dadiji (my grandmother) to supervise and cook the afternoon meal. With a thumping heart and heavy feet she walked towards the kitchen. Tears were in her eyes. Ramus (the servant) noticed and closed the kitchen door. He suggested that he would cook the best meal he knew how on her behalf. The same day she wrote to her father to take her back for a month. She tried very hard to learn many dishes, not for the sake of cooking, but to win the heart of her darling and his family. She did so and made sure that her daughters – servants or no servants – must cook something special at least once a week so that they would not be in the same position when they married.

When we were little, we used to play a cooking game during the school holidays called 'Halkuliya' and the meaning we understood was 'work done together'. All the boys would go around the garden to pick the wood and bricks. Of course we couldn't borrow the wood or coal or use the kitchen fire otherwise it wouldn't be 'Halkuliya'. It was different to borrow flour, ghee, oil, potatoes, onions and utensils from mother and aunties. When we had collected everything we would place three bricks to make a stove. My brothers would make the fire and go with our little sisters to hunt for more wood and large leaves. They would pick vegetables from our garden secretly so that 'mali' (gardener) would not see them. The girls would start cooking. I had older girl cousins who would always make me sit and fry and it worked very nicely too because at 7 year's old I was happy to co-operate. I would do just as I was told (I wanted to be highly appreciated) but on the other hand I secretly

Introduction

passed some of the cooked food to my brothers and my little sisters who were working so hard in my opinion. At the end everyone would sit down and the food was served on large leaves. This was the most wonderful and satisfying food in our eyes. Pakora, puri, puri waleé aloo, mixed vegetables and kheer (rice pudding) were the dishes we most often attempted to do.

Once when I was giving a cookery lesson, one of the students asked me, "Why do we add tomatoes and fry until all the liquid has been absorbed and then add yogurt and then water. Why don't we just add everything together at one time?" I answered her, "By adding at different times and frying it each time we fry one stage further. If we added everything at once we won't be frying, we will be boiling." She was satisfied and said, "How scientific!"

A Few Points to Remember

The most important thing is to read the recipe through completely at least once before actually starting to cook. Don't be put off by the large amount of ingredients in each recipe. Most of these are standard spices kept in your cupboard. The following are a few handy hints while cooking:

1 **BREAD:** Frying bread or other things:-
   (a) When frying bread do not roll in dry flour as it burns and discolours the cooking fat. Use oil instead of dry flour.
   (b) Do not throw bread in the middle of the hot oil pan otherwise the hot oil will spit and splash. This can be dangerous. Slip a puri or bhutoora, katchori, breadroll, samosa etc, gently from the edge of the frying pan.
   (c) When rolling a chapati or paratha do not use too much dry flour because it burns quicker and gives a dark, burnt look to the bread.

2 **BURNT DISH:** If you have burnt your dish, do not scrape from the bottom. Place the top of the dish into a clean saucepan and carry on cooking.

3 **CAULIFLOWER:** A white coloured cauliflower is always fresher, tender and sweeter than a yellow one.
How to grate? Wash a whole cauliflower, take a knife and start slicing about 2mm thick along the top. When you reach the stems then obviously grating with a grater will save your time.

4 **COOKING TIME:** I cannot give exact cooking times because a lot depends on the quantity and quality (tenderness and age) of the food you want to cook.

5 **CUMIN:**
   (a) When added to hot oil, takes it only 2 seconds to brown.
   (b) Roasting:- place a dry flat frying pan on a medium heat, add the cumin seeds. Stir until golden brown. Turn the heat off but keep on stirring. Leave to cool. Coarsely grind and keep in an airtight jar.

6 **DOUGH:** One must be wondering what is soft, hard or stiff

A Few Points to Remember

dough, therefore I have given the quantity of water but at times you have to slightly adjust the quantity of the water because it depends on the texture and moisture of the flour.

7　***FROZEN FOOD:*** Most of the cooked Indian food can be frozen unless stated otherwise (in the recipe).

    (a) If frozen foods are used in any of the recipes then naturally the dish should not be re-frozen as some of its contents will have been frozen twice (it does not apply for a short term freezing). If using frozen peas (for example) freeze the food and add the peas when reheating.

    (b) If any dish has been frozen, then sufficient time should be allowed for the food to be completely defrosted before reheating.

8　***GARLIC AND GINGER:*** Always peel and wash before chopping or grinding.

9　***GARAM MASALA:*** Always sprinkle a little ground garam masala before serving a dish so that it retains its pleasent aroma. Whole garam masala (cloves, peppercorns, cinnamon stick and black cardomon) retains its fragrance for a long time therefore I add them at the beginning especially in a dish which contains sauce.

10　***HOTNESS OF FOOD:*** It is difficult to say how hot a dish is because it depends on individual taste. One dish may be hot for you but not for me or visa versa. The thing which is making your dish hot is red and green chilli therefore increase or decrease the quantity of chillies according to your taste. Food will be delicious even with just a pinch of ground red chilli.

11　***LEMON:*** Always add lemon juice at the end once the lentils, vegetables and meat are cooked and tender otherwise they will take longer to cook.

12　***LENTILS:*** In India lentil or dal have quite a runny constituency. Thick and overcooked lentil loses its flavour.

13　***LID:*** Why close the lid on a saucepan while cooking:

    (a　The food cooks quicker.

    (b) The food retains its nutrition value.

A Few Points to Remember

(c) The fragrance of the spices isn't lost.

(d) The food is cooked in the steam.

14 ***MEASUREMENT:*** All teaspoons are level.

    Onion size: (a)   Small 50 g/2 oz

                    (b)   Medium size 100 g/4 oz

                    (c)   Large 200 g/7 oz

15 ***MICROWAVE OVEN:*** The popularity of a microwave oven is increasing rapidly. It can be used to speed up defrosting. It is a marvellous gadget to reheat cooked food especially rice dishes.

16 ***MILK:*** Always rinse your saucepan before adding milk to boil. It will prevent milk sticking to the pan.

17 ***MUSTARD SEEDS:*** When frying cover the pan to avoid spitting.

18 ***OIL:***

(a) How to check that the oil is hot? Slip a little dough or batter or a thin slice of onion into the hot oil, if it sizzles and comes up at once the oil is hot.

(b) Left over fried oil:- Keep it separate and use only for frying.

(c) Never fry vegetables in oil in which you have fried fish, meat and chicken.

(d) Always use fresh oil for dishes (e.g. currys, rice etc).

19 ***ONION:*** Always wash onions after peeling. If they make you cry soak them in cold water for a little while or peel them in water or after peeling cut in half and leave them aside for 10 minutes before you start chopping.

20 ***POPPY SEEDS:*** How to clean and grind :- They are often quite dirty therefore soak them in lukewarm water, drain, dry and grind them in a coffee grinder.

21 ***RICE:***

(a) To see if any remaining water is left after cooking rice, tip the pan a little but do not stir. Place pan back on a high heat and dry off any remaining water. Close the lid and leave for at least 5 minutes before serving.

(b) Stir cooked rice gently with a fork before serving.

A Few Points to Remember

(c) It is very delicate when cooked therefore is best eaten immediately.

22 **SALT:** Indians take more salt through savoury yogurt dishes and salty lemon squash etc especially during the summer so that they can replace the salt which they have lost.

23 **SPICES:** Grind your own spices and store in a jar e.g. coriander, cumin and garam masala. This is because:-

      (a)   The spices are cleaned.

      (b)   They are fresh and whole spices store better.

      (c)   They are pure and not a mixture of other spices.

      (d)   They are full of fragrance;

24 **TYMOL SEEDS:** Tymol seeds contain quite a lot of dirt. Therefore either clean them or soak and drain in a strainer before using.

25 **UTENSILS:** For cooking, a saucepan or a frying pan should be heavy. As much as possible use stainless steel or enamel-ware saucepans because some of the ingredients contain acidity like tamarind, lemon, mango, cooking apples etc.

26 **WHOLE SPICES:** I like to add cloves, cinnamon, black pepper and black cardamoms in a curry while frying onions. Whole spices retain their fragrance for longer periods than garam masala (after grinding the above spices one makes garam masala). In India most people are habitual in keeping aside whole spices while eating their meal but if by mistake you chew them whole they are very strong. Therefore if you or your guest are not sure please leave the whole spices completely out of your dish (for this purpose the whole spices have been asterisked* in most recipes) and instead increase 2.5 ml/ ½ tsp garam masala in your recipe.

Miscellaneous

Garam Masala
Ghee
Khoya
Paneer
Potatoes boiled in their jackets
Roasted Cumin
Sambar Masala
Tamarind Pulp
Yoghurt

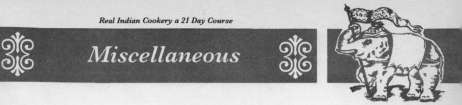

Miscellaneous

Garam Masala

Make your own garam masala. There is no comparison between garam masala bought from a shop and that made at home. One can keep the home made garam masala in an airtight container for at least at least three months without losing its aroma.

Ingredients:	Metric	Imperial	American
Black cardamom, use only seeds	*25 g*	*1 oz*	*1 oz*
Black peppercorns	*25 g*	*1 oz*	*1 oz*
Cloves	*25 g*	*1 oz*	*1 oz*
Cinnamon stick, break into small pieces	*25 g*	*1 oz*	*1 oz*

Grind the above ingredients in a coffee grinder until it resembles the consistency of powder.

Miscellaneous

Ghee
(Clarified butter)

Some families in Northern India cook in ghee as opposed to oil. This is actually very fattening. However, sweets especially taste a lot better if ghee is used.

Ingredients:	Metric	Imperial	American
Butter	500 g	1 lb 2 oz	18 oz
Muslin cloth			

1 Put the butter in a large saucepan and boil, stirring, until all the butter has melted.
2 When the solids (whey) appear at the bottom and the clear part (ghee) is at the top, reduce the heat to low. Keep on stirring until it is light brown. Turn off the heat and keep stirring so that it does not boil over. Allow to cool slightly.
3 Put a muslin cloth over a container or jar and pour the contents of the saucepan into the cloth so that the ghee strains through into the container.
4 Squeeze the remaining ghee from the muslin cloth and discard the contents of the cloth. Let the ghee cool down and then place the lid on the container and keep aside until required.
5 The cloth can be re-used after washing. Ghee can be kept for months in an airtight container.

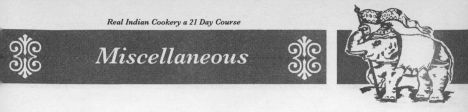

Miscellaneous

Khoya

Traditional Way of Making Khoya:

Ingredients:	Metric	Imperial	American
Milk, gold top	1.1 ltr.	2 pt	5 cups

Place the milk in a large heavy-bottomed saucepan and bring to the boil. Reduce the heat to medium-low and keep stirring until it solidifies. It will take about 2 hours.

Quick Way Of Making Khoya:

Ingredients:	Metric	Imperial	American
Full cream milk powder	50 g	2 oz	1/2 cup
Ghee, melted	2 tsp	10 ml	2 tsp
Milk, lukewarm	30 ml	2 tbsp	2 tbsp

Combine all the above ingredients in a bowl, mix it and form into a ball (like soft dough).

 Miscellaneous

Paneer
(Indian Cheese)

Indian people like to make cheese at home. Indian cheese differs in taste from English and overseas cheese. One can fry paneer and it becomes softer and spongy when cooked.

Ingredients:	Metric	Imperial	American
Milk (preferably gold top)	1.1 ltr.	2 pt	5 cups
Lemon juice	30 ml	2 tbsp	2 tbsp

Heat the milk in a heavy bottomed saucepan, as it comes to the boil add the lemon juice (if needed add more) so that the milk separates into curd and whey. Leave to set for 5 minutes. Do not throw away the whey because it contains minerals and can be used in curries instead of water. This also adds an extra taste to a curry.

Line a strainer with a cloth, strain the milk and squeeze out the excess whey and fold the cloth around the paneer to form a square (about 4" square). Put on an upturned plate and place a heavy weight on top to squeeze out any excess whey. Leave for about 4 hours to set. For most curries cut the paneer into small pieces (1.0 cm/½" square) and fry them in a deep frying pan (on a medium heat) until light golden brown. When the paneer is used in a sweet recipe do not fry.

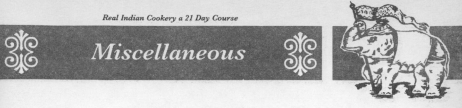

Miscellaneous

Potatoes Boiled In Jackets

Potatoes are the cheapest commodity and are used abundantly in Indian cooking. We usually like to boil potatoes in their jackets and then peel them.

Ingredients:	Metric	Imperial	American
Potatoes, washed	*500 g*	*1 lb 2 oz*	*18 oz*
Water	*1.2 ltrs.*	*2 pints*	*5 cups*

Place the potato and the water in a large saucepan. Bring to the boil, reduce the heat to medium low, close the lid, and cook for 20-25 minutes or until tender.

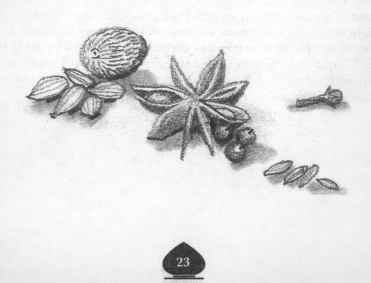

Miscellaneous

Roasted Cumin

When in a recipe I say ground cumin, it refers to roasted ground cumin.

Ingredients:	Metric	Imperial	American
Cumin cleaned	*50 g*	*2 oz*	*¹/₄ cup*

Heat a tawa or flat frying pan on a medium-low heat. Place the cumin on it and keep on turning them over for 2 minutes or until brown. Cool and grind coarsely. Keep in an airtight jar. For best results use within a month of grinding.

Miscellaneous

Sambar Masala

Ingredients:	Metric	Imperial	American
Coconut desicated (or freshly grated)	50 g	2 oz	¼ cup
Oil	15 ml	1 tbsp	1 tbsp
Whole coriander, cleaned	15 ml	1 tbsp	1 tbsp
Urid ki dal, cleaned	10 ml	2 tsp	2 tsp
Gram dal (split yellow peas), cleaned	10 ml	2 tsp	2 tsp
Fenugreek seeds	5 ml	1 tsp	1 tsp
Whole small dried red chilli	4	4	4

Heat the oil in a flat frying pan on a medium-low heat and roast all the ingredients for 5 minutes or until light brown. Cool, grind to a fine paste. Keep any remaining Sambar Masala in an airtight jar for next use.

Miscellaneous

Extracting Tamarind Pulp

Tamarind trees are large and shady and that is why they are planted on the roadside. During the heat of summer the people, cows and goats etc. take shelter under them. We used to pick unripe tamarind on our way to school and eat them with salt and pepper. They are very sour (tart) and one cannot eat too many. When ripe, the stones are removed and after drying they are packed in bars. One can keep them for at least a year. Tamarind is full of iron.

Ingredients:	Metric	Imperial	American
Dry tamarind, soaked overnight or boiled in 300 ml/11 fl oz water for 15 minutes on a medium-low heat	*100 g*	*4 oz*	*4 oz*

Extract pulp (sieve) from soaked or boiled and cooked tamarind and throw away the seeds and the sticks etc. (the waste shouldn't exceed 15 ml/1 tbsp). I use 300 ml/11 fl oz/1¼ cups of cold water to extract the pulp and never add more than 50 ml/3 tbsp or 60 ml/4tbsp water at a time to sieve pulp.

Miscellaneous

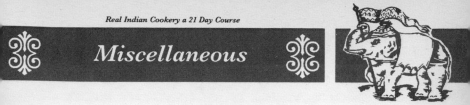

Yoghurt
(Home made natural yoghurt)

To start making home made natural yoghurt one needs thick natural yoghurt from a supermarket. After that use home made yoghurt as culture. After a month I restart the process.

Ingredients:	Metric	Imperial	American
Milk, lukewarm	*575 ml*	*1 pt*	*2½ cups*
Culture from a thick natural yoghurt, mix with a little milk until smooth	*15 ml*	*1 tbsp*	*1 tbsp*

Place the milk in a saucepan or dish with tight lid. Mix the culture in the lukewarm milk, close the lid and leave it to set in an airing cupboard for 8 hours. When set (check it) keep it in the refrigerator for at least 3-4 hours before using.

Today's cooking consists of
a main dish and one of the most
popular breads of India. This is
combined with egg curry which can
also be
served with rice.
(When serving with rice; spread the
sauce over the plain rice, arrange egg
pieces on the top and garnish with
chopped coriander leaves and garam
masala.) Try also to prepare a
delicious Indian Sweet to finish your
meal.

DAY 1

Undé Ki Sabji
(Egg Curry – My Mother's style)

Serves: 4-6

My mother created this hearty dish. It was one of the dishes I cooked for my prize winning entry in the Shajhanpur district competition. It is of medium hotness. (Undé means egg.)

1st Stage: making the paste

Ingredients:	Metric	Imperial	American
Eggs, hard boiled, shelled and cut into halves lengthwise.	6	6	6
Oil or Ghee	150 ml	5 fl oz	²/₃ cup
Cumin Seeds	5 ml	1 tsp	1 tsp
Medium onion, finely chopped	1	1	1
*Cloves	4	4	4
*Peppercorns	4	4	4
*Cinnamon Stick	2.5 cm	1"	1"
*Black Cardamon	1	1	1
Bay leaves	4	4	4

2nd Stage: for the blended paste

	Metric	Imperial	American
Large garlic clove, coarsely chopped	4	4	4
Medium onion, coarsely chopped	3	3	3
Fresh ginger, coarsely chopped	2.5 cm	1"	1"

Combine the garlic, onion and ginger in a blender and blend with 30 ml/ 2 tbsp water to make a smooth paste.

	Metric	Imperial	American
Poppy seeds, ground finely in a grinder	25 g	1 oz	1 oz
Coconut desiccated (or fresh), ground very finely in a grinder	75 g	3 oz	¹/₃ cup
Ground coriander	10 ml	2 tsp	2 tsp

Ground turmeric	2.5 ml	$^1/_2$ tsp	$^1/_2$ tsp
Ground red chilli	2.5 ml	$^1/_2$ tsp	$^1/_2$ tsp
Garam masala	5 ml	1 tsp	1 tsp
Salt to taste			
Tomatoes, tinned	400 g	14 oz	1 cup
Lemon juice	15 ml	1 tbsp	1 tbsp

To Garnish

Garam Masala	2.5 ml	$^1/_2$ tsp	$^1/_2$ tsp
Green coriander			
leaves, chopped	15 ml	1 tbsp	1 tbsp
Small green chilli,			
chopped (optional)	1	1	1

Cooking Time: 1 hour

1 Heat the oil in a large heavy-bottomed saucepan and brown the cumin seeds. Add the chopped onion, the whole spices and fry gently until golden brown on medium heat.
2 Stir in the blended paste and fry for five minutes.
3 Put in the ground poppy seeds and fry for two minutes.
4 Then add the ground coconut and fry everything for a further few minutes until golden brown.
5 Stir in the ground spices (coriander, turmeric, red chilli, garam masala), salt and tomatoes. Fry until all the liquid has been absorbed and the oil appears on the surface of the mixture.
6 Pour in 45 ml/ 3 tbsp of water and fry until all the water is absorbed. Repeat this twice so that the spices can mature in the sauce.
7 Add 250 ml/ 9 fl oz/ 1 cup water and the lemon juice. Bring to boil, reduce the heat to low, close the lid and simmer for 3 minutes.

Garnish Suggestion:

Pour the hot sauce in a serving dish. Place the eggs on the top and sprinkle over the garnish before serving.

Serving Suggestion:

Serve hot with rice, puri, dahibara and potato beans dish.

Puri

Makes: 20

Puri is probably the most popular bread and is used all over India. It is easy, quick to make and suitable for serving to guests. An average adult will consume about 4 puris.

Making the dough:

Ingredients:	Metric	Imperial	American
Brown chapati flour	*500 g*	*1 lb 2 oz*	*18 oz*
Oil	*30 ml*	*2 tbsp*	*2 tbsp*
Salt	*large pinch*	*⅛ tsp*	*⅛ tsp*
Water, luke warm	*275 ml*	*9.5 fl oz*	*1 cup*

1 Place the flour in a bowl.
2 Rub in the oil and salt thoroughly.
3 Knead the dough with warm water for 2-5 minutes or until the dough is springy and satiny.
4 Cover and leave for 30 minutes.

Frying the Puri:
Cooking Time: 30 minutes

1 Pour enough oil into your frying pan to fill to three-quarters full.
2 Heat the oil on medium heat. While the oil is heating divide the dough into 20 equal portions.
3 Take a portion of dough and roll it into a ball on the palm of the hands. Flatten it, place a few drops of oil on the rolling board and roll it into a thin (5 mm/ ¼") round with a rolling pin.
4 Slip a puri into the hot oil from the edge of the pan. Gently but swiftly press the puri all over with a slotted spoon and it will rise like a balloon.
5 Fry both sides golden brown. I roll another puri while one is frying.

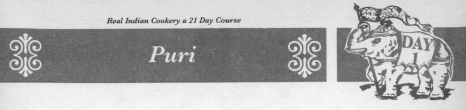

Puri

Serving Suggestion:

Serve hot with a meal. Puri goes superbly with any sort of vegetables, lentil or yoghurt dish.

Coconut and Chocolate Barfi

Makes: 24

This sweet is very popular with coconut lovers and children.
The yellow and brown colours look very attractive and
stimulate the appetite.

Ingredients:	Metric	Imperial	American
Full cream milk powder	125 g	4 oz	1 cup
Fresh or tinned cream,			
whisked to thicken	150 g	6 oz	$^2/_3$ cup
Ghee	5 ml	1 tsp	1 tsp
Ground green cardamom	1.5 ml	$^1/_4$ tsp	$^1/_4$ tsp

Place the above ingredients in a bowl. Mix thoroughly and set it to
one side.

Desiccated sweet coconut	75 g	3 oz	$^1/_3$ cup
Ghee	10 ml	2 tsp	2 tsp
Sugar	75 g	3 oz	$^1/_3$ cup
Ground green cardamom	5 ml	1 tsp	1 tsp
Colouring, yellow	2.5 ml	$^1/_2$ tsp	$^1/_2$ tsp
Plate, greased	1	1	1
Milk chocolate			
(for cake covering)	100 g	4 oz	$^1/_2$ cup

Cooking Time: 20 minutes

1 Place the coconut and the ghee in a saucepan and fry it light
   brown on a low heat.
2 Add the milk powder mixture, sugar, green cardamon and
   colouring. Cook this on medium-low heat.
3 Stir thoroughly until the mixture thickens sufficiently to set; (this is
   normally five minutes after the mixture seems to come away
   from the pan) on setting, the mixture should hold together and
   be non-sticky.
4 Make a ball with the palm of your hands. Place it on a plate and
   flatten it in a square shape about 1 cm/ $^1/_2$" thick.

Coconut and Chocolate Barfi

 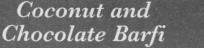 

5   Break the milk chocolate into small pieces in a small bowl and melt over a saucepan containing boiling water.

6   Pour the milk chocolate over the coconut barfi.

7   NB. Stages 5 and 6 are optional, it is not necessary to add the chocolate layer.

8   Leave to set for 3-4 hours.

9   Cut into square or diamond shapes (side about 3 cm).

Serving suggestion:

Serve cold after a meal or at tea with samosa, pakora, mathi or dalmod etc.

DAY
2

Today I have decided to include a meat dish from the West of India. I am also going to introduce to you the most simple bread eaten daily in India. This is called Chapati. No Indian meal is complete without a yoghurt compliment therefore also learn how to make the simple and delicious rayta.

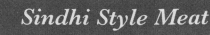

Sindhi Style Meat

Serve: 4

This is a medium hot dish with the exotic flavour of fenugreek leaves.

Ingredients:	Metric	Imperial	American
Mutton or lamb, boned, cut into 2.5 cm/ 1" pieces, fat trimmed off and washed	*500g*	*1lb 2 oz*	*18 oz*
Oil or ghee	*75 ml*	*5 tbsp*	*5 tbsp*
Large garlic cloves, crushed	*5*	*5*	*5*
Fresh ginger, finely chopped	*4 cm*	*1.5"*	*1.5"*
Medium onion, finely chopped	*2*	*2*	*2*
Bay leaves	*2*	*2*	*2*
Ground coriander	*10 ml*	*2 tsp*	*2 tsp*
Garam masala	*5 ml*	*1 tsp*	*1 tsp*
Ground turmeric	*2.5 ml*	*1/2 tsp*	*1/2 tsp*
Red chilli	*2.5 ml*	*1/2 tsp*	*1/2 tsp*
Salt to taste			
Fenugreek leaves, chopped (dried methi leaves 1 tbsp)	*45 ml*	*3 tbsp*	*3 tbsp*
Canned tomatoes	*400 g*	*14 oz*	*2 cups*
Natural yogurt	*150 g*	*5 oz*	*2/3 cup*
To Garnish			
Garam masala	*2.5 ml*	*1/2 tsp*	*1/2 tsp*
Green coriander leaves,chopped	*15 ml*	*1 tbsp*	*1 tbsp*
Small green chilli, chopped	*1*	*1*	*1*

Cooking time: 1 hour

1 Heat the oil in a heavy-bottomed saucepan on a medium heat and fry chopped onion until light brown.
2 Add the bay leaves, garlic, and ginger, and fry until golden brown.
3 Add the meat pieces and fry until light brown.
4 Stir in the coriander, garam masala, turmeric, red chilli, salt and tomatoes, and cook until all the liquid has been absorbed.

Sindhi Style Meat

5 Add fenugreek leaves and yoghurt and cook until oil appears at the
        top.
6 Pour 150 ml/ ½ pt/ ⅔ cup of water. Reduce the heat to low, close
        the lid and simmer until meat is tender.
7 Sprinkle over the garnish before serving.

Serving suggestion:
Serve hot with plain rice, puri and cauliflower.

Chapati

Makes: 9

Chapati is also very commonly known as *roti* or *phulka*. Chapati is a fairly easy bread to cook and digest therefore it is eaten daily in India. It can be made from plain white flour or brown chapati flour (if you cannot get hold of the latter mix equal quantities of wholemeal and plain flour). I prefer chapati flour as it contains more roughage.

Ingredients:	Metric	Imperial	American
Chapati flour	*250 g*	*9 oz*	*1 cup*
Lukewarm water	*150 ml*	*¹/₄ pt*	*²/₃ cup*
Butter or ghee to smear			

Making the dough:

Keep aside a handful of flour for rolling-out. Place the chapati flour in a bowl.

Mix in the water to make a soft dough. Knead for two minutes or until the dough is springy and satiny. Cover and leave aside for 10 minutes.

Making the chapati:
Cooking Time: 25 minutes

1 Divide the dough into 9 equal portions.
2 Take a portion of dough and roll it into a ball in the palm of your hands. Flatten, and dust in dry flour.
3 Roll out on a rolling board into a thin round circle.
4 Heat a flat frying pan on medium heat. Place the chapati on it and cook for about one minute, turn over and lightly cook on the other side (making sure all the edges are cooked – it will be approximately 1 minute). Turn again and press the chapati gently with a clean cloth and it will rise like a balloon (it will take 30-45 seconds). I roll my next chapati while one is cooking. Smear one face of the cooked chapati with butter or ghee(5 ml/ 1 tsp).

Serving Suggestion:

Serve hot with all sorts of curries.

Tomato, Cucumber and Onion Rayta

Serves: 4-6

This is one of the most popular yoghurt dishes in India, and is incredibly easy and quick to make. This rayta goes excellently with most Indian dishes.

Preparing the rayta:

Ingredients:	Metric	Imperial	American
Natural yoghurt, chilled and whisked until smooth	500 g	18 fl oz	2 cups
Tomatoes washed and cut into 1.2 cm/ 0.5" pieces	150 g	5 oz	5 oz
Small onion, finely chopped	1	1	1
Cucumber, washed and cut into 1.2 cm/ 0.5" pieces	1/2	1/2	1/2
Salt to taste			
Ground roasted cumin	2.5 ml	1/2 tsp	1/2 tsp

To garnish:

	Metric	Imperial	American
Ground roasted cumin	2.5 ml	1/2 tsp	1/2 tsp
Green coriander leaves, chopped	15 ml	1 tbsp	1 tbsp
Small green chilli chopped	1	1	1

Preparation time: 10 minutes

1 Place the whisked yoghurt in a deep bowl. Mix in the salt and ground cumin.
2 A few minutes before you want to eat add the tomatoes, onions, and cucumber pieces.
3 Mix them thoroughly.
4 Sprinkle over the garnish before serving.

Serving Suggestions:

Serve chilled with a meal.

Today one of the most popular starters/snacks - samosas with tamarind chutney is awaiting you. Samosas are consumed all over the world. Even the supermarkets could not resist the temptation of selling them. If you follow the recipe carefully you will be able to produce more delicious fresh and crispy samosas. Not only that, but the money you save by making them yourself will be enough to treat yourself to another of my cookery books!

You can also learn how to make another popular sweet called jalebi.

Vegetable Samosa

DAY 3

Makes: 16

Vegetable samosa is one of the most delicious and popular snacks, among both vegetarians and non-vegetarians. The dough can be prepared by two methods, both are given below.

Preparing the dough:

Method 1

Ingredients:	Metric	Imperial	American
Plain flour, sifted	200 g	7 oz	1 cup
Lemon juice	5 ml	1 tsp	1 tsp
Salt	small pinch	small pinch	small pinch
Water, luke warm	75 ml	3 fl oz	5 tbsp

Place 150g/ 5 oz/ 1 ¼ cups of flour in a bowl. Mix in the lemon juice and the salt. Knead the dough with the water for 5 minutes or until the dough is springy and satiny. Cover and set on one side for 10 minutes.

Method 2

Ingredients:	Metric	Imperial	American
Plain flour, sifted	150 g	5 oz	1 ¼ cups
Oil	15 ml	1 tbsp	1 tbsp
Salt	small pinch	small pinch	small pinch
Water, lukewarm	75 ml	3 fl oz	5 tbsp

Place the sifted flour in a bowl. Mix in the oil and the salt. Knead the dough with the water for 5 minutes or until the dough is springy and satiny. Cover and set on one side for 10 minutes.

Preparing the filling:

Ingredients:	Metric	Imperial	American
Oil	45 ml	3 tbsp	3 tbsp
Cumin seeds	5 ml	1 tsp	1 tsp

Vegetable Samosa

DAY 3

Ingredients:	Metric	Imperial	American
Potatoes, boiled in jackets, peeled then diced.	500 g	1 lb 2 oz	18 oz
Peas (frozen or fresh-shelled)	250 g	9 oz	9 oz
Garam masala	5 ml	1 tsp	1 tsp
Ground roasted cumin	5 ml	1 tsp	1 tsp
Ground ginger	2.5 ml	1/2 tsp	1/2 tsp
Ground red chilli	2.5 ml	1/2 tsp	1/2 tsp
Ground turmeric	2.5 ml	1/2 tsp	1/2 tsp
Salt to taste			
Lemon juice	30 ml	2 tbsp	2 tbsp
Sugar	15 ml	1 tbsp	1 tbsp
Green coriander leaves, chopped	60 ml	4 tbsp	4 tbsp
Small green chilli, chopped	1	1	1
Oil to fry and smear			

Cooking time: 20 minutes

1 Heat the oil in a deep frying pan on medium heat and brown the cumin seeds.
2 Add the potato pieces and fry for 10 minutes or until light golden brown.
3 Stir in the ground spices, salt and the frozen peas and cook until tender.
4 Mix the juice and the sugar and cook for 2 minutes.
5 Turn the heat off, add the coriander leaves and the green chilli and mix them well.
6 Leave to cool on one side (and divide into 16 equal portions).

Preparing the pastry: Method 1

1 Make a runny batter using 15 ml/ 1 tbsp flour and 15-30 ml/ 1-2 tbsp water and set to one side.
2 Divide the dough into 8 equal portions.
3 Roll each piece into a ball in the palm of your hands.
4 Dust them in flour then roll them into small circles.

Vegetable Samosa

5 Sprinkle some flour on the rolling board, place a circle on the board, smear the top with oil, sprinkle some flour on it and place another circle on top, repeat this so that 4 circles lie on top of each other.

5 Sprinkle some flour on top then roll the whole thing out thinly.

6 Heat a flat frying pan on medium heat. Reduce to low heat and place the rolled circles on it. Bake for 10-20 seconds or until dry, turn over and remove the first layer, immediately turn over again and remove the second layer, turn over and remove the third and forth layers.

7 Place them on a cooling tray and cover with a tea cloth.

8 Repeat with the rest of the dough.

9 Cut the rounds in half.

10 Take one half, by bringing the corners towards each other let the flat edge meet and overlap in the centre, forming a cone shape.

11 Brush one side of the overlap with batter and stick down firmly.

12 Fill the cone with potato mixture.

13 Brush the edges with batter and firmly seal the cone.

At this stage the samosas can be frozen and freshly deep fried when one wants to serve. With practice this method is quicker and the pastry is very fine.

Method 2

1 Divide the dough into eight equal portions.

2 Take a portion of dough and roll it into a ball in the palm of your hands, flatten it, place a few drops of oil on the rolling board and thinly roll into a large circle.

3 Cut the circle in half.

4 Make a cone, fill and seal as in method 1 except this time sealing with water.

5 Pinch the arched edge with your fingers to give an attractive pattern.

6 These should be fried first before freezing and reheated under a grill.

Vegetable Samosa

Frying the samosas:
Frying time: 20 minutes

Heat the oil in a deep frying pan on medium heat.
Gently slip 5 or 6 samosas into the hot oil, reduce heat to medium-low and fry until crispy light golden brown on all sides (do not fry too quickly).

Serving suggestion:

Serve hot with tamarind chutney, gulab jamun or rasmalai at tea.

❧❦ Tamarind Chutney ❧❦

DAY 3

Fills 1.5 kg (1 lb) (450 g) jam jars

Tamarind chutney is not only delicious, but an excellent
source of iron and other minerals. It will keep for a long
time in an air tight container if a clean dry spoon is used
to take it out. The chutney is acidic, so while cooking and
eating use a wooden or stainless steel spoon. You will find the
chutney to be quite hot.

Ingredients:	Metric	Imperial	American
Dry tamarind, soaked overnight	100 g	4 oz	4 oz
*Water	300 ml	1/2 pt	1 1/8 cup
Jaggery or sugar	250 g	9 oz	1 cup
Garam masala	5 ml	1 tsp	1 tsp
Ground roasted cumin	5 ml	1 tsp	1 tsp
Ground red chilli	2.5 ml	1/2 tsp	1/2 tsp
Salt (or black salt) to taste			
Raisins	50 g	2 oz	1/2 cup
Dried dates, pitted and finely sliced	5	5	5

*If you are unable to soak your tamarind overnight, boil it in the
   300 ml water for 15 minutes on low heat.

1 Extract the pulp from soaked/boiled tamarind by seiving it
   thoroughly. Through away the seeds and the sticks (the waste
   should not exceed 1 tbsp). I use 300 ml/ 0.5 pt of cold water to
   extract the pulp, never adding more than 50-60 ml at a time
   to seive the pulp.

2 *Cooking time:* **15 minutes**
   Place the pulp on high heat with the sugar and all the ground
   spices. Bring to the boil and reduce the heat to medium-low
   and cook for 10 minutes.

3 Add the dates and the raisins and cook for a further 2 or 3 minutes.

Tamarind Chutney

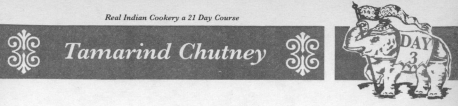

4 Let the chutney cool down, (do not close the lid while this is happening), then put it into the empty jars.

Serving suggestion:
Serve cold with a main meal or with samosa, pakora, kabab, breadroll etc. at tea time.

Jalebi

Serves: 4-6

Jalebi is a delightful Indian sweet. Every Sunday we used to have it for breakfast. Some people like to eat jalebi with milk and yoghurt.

Making the batter:

Ingredients:	Metric	Imperial	American
Dried yeast	*5 ml*	*1 tsp*	*1 tsp*
Water, tepid	*45 ml*	*3 tbsp*	*3 tbsp*

Place the yeast and water into a small bowl. Beat with a fork, cover and leave in a warm place for 30 minutes. It should rise and foam up.

Plain flour, sifted	*100 g*	*4 oz*	*1/2 cup*
Water, tepid	*150 g*	*5 oz*	*2/3 cup*
Lemon juice	*5 ml*	*1 tsp*	*1 tsp*

1 Mix the sifted flour and the lemon juice into the risen yeast.
2 Gradually add the water to make a smooth batter.
3 Cover and leave for 1 hour; it should rise double in size.

Preparing the syrup:

Water	*200 ml*	*7 fl oz*	*1 cup*
Sugar	*150 g*	*5 oz*	*2/3 cup*
Colouring, yellow	*5 ml*	*1 tsp*	*1 tsp*

1 Place the water and the sugar in a saucepan.
2 Bring to the boil on medium heat
3 Stir in the colour and reduce the heat to very low and let it simmer while you make the jalebi.

Cooking time: 45 minutes

1 Heat a mixture of ghee and oil (equal quantities) in a deep frying pan on medium heat.

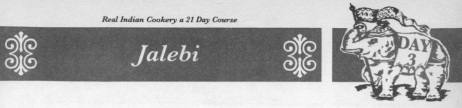

Jalebi

2 Mix the batter with a fork.

3 (I use an empty, cleaned and dried washing-up liquid bottle, but one can use an icing pump bag with a medium nozzle.) Take the lid or cap off the bottle. Place a funnel on the bottle and pour in the batter. Place the cap back.

4 Hold the bottle upside down, 15 cm/6" above the hot fat, gently press the bottle but swiftly move your hand to form the batter into coiled circles or spirals in the hot fat.

5 Fry 4 or 5 jalebis together until golden brown on both sides.

6 Take them out with a slotted spoon, dip in the hot syrup and let them soak for 30 seconds, turn them over and let them soak for a further 15 seconds. Drain and remove all the jalebies from the syrup and put them on a cooking tray.

7 Repeat until all the batter is used.

Serving suggestion:

Serve hot at breakfast, after a meal or as a sweet snack. The jalebis can be reheated under a grill.

DAY
4

Today let me take you to the North of India. Have a taste of Punjab's Khatéwalé Kabuli Chunna (chickpeas) and Bhutoora (bread). These mouth watering dishes can convert anyone to be a fan of Indian food. They are popular all over India and are suitable for all occasions.

Also awaiting you today is Prawn Pulao prepared in an East Indian (Bengal) style.

Prawn Pulao

Serves 4-6

This delicious combination of layers of rice and prawns originates from Bengal. It is a delicate dish and best eaten the moment it is prepared. You will find it to be of medium hotness.

Preparing the rice:

Ingredients:	Metric	Imperial	American
Rice (Patna or Basmati) cleaned, washed and drained	225 g	8 oz	1 cup
Ghee	75 ml	5 tbsp	5 tbsp
Cumin seeds	5 ml	1 tsp	1 tsp
*Cloves	4	4	4
*Peppercorns	4	4	4
Bay leaves	2	2	2
*Cardamon	1	1	1
*Cinnamon stick	1.2 cm	1/2 "	1/2 "
Garam masala	2.5 ml	1/2 tsp	1/2 tsp
Water	400 ml	14 fl oz	2 cups
Milk	50 ml	2 fl oz	3 1/2 tbsp
Salt to taste			

Cooking Time: 25 minutes

1 Heat the ghee in a large heavy bottomed saucepan, brown the cumin seeds and then add the whole spices and the rice. Stir the mixture for two minutes until it no longer sticks.
2 Add the garam masala, salt and water; bring to boil on high heat.
3 Reduce the heat to minimum. Cover the pan and simmer for 15 minutes. (Remember not to stir it or lift the lid before the cooking time.)

Preparing the prawn:

Ingredients:	Metric	Imperial	American
Large peeled prawns fresh or frozen	250 g	9 oz	1 cup
Oil	75 ml	5 tbsp	5 tbsp
Large garlic cloves, crushed	3	3	3

Ingredients:	Metric	Imperial	American
Medium onion, thinly sliced	1	1	1
Ginger	2.5 cm	1"	1"
Ground coriander	5 ml	1 tsp	1 tsp
Ground roasted cumin	5 ml	1 tsp	1 tsp
Ground red chilli	2.5 ml	1/2 tsp	1/2 tsp
Ground turmeric	2.5 ml	1/2 tsp	1/2 tsp
Tomatoes, tinned	230 g	8 oz	1 cup
Natural yoghurt	150 g	5 oz	2/3 cup
Desiccated coconut or fresh (grated)	50 g	2 oz	1/4 cup
Salt to taste			

To Garnish:

Green coriander leaves, chopped	15 ml	1 tbsp	1 tbsp
Garam masala	5 ml	1 tsp	1 tsp
Small green chilli, chopped	1	1	1

Cooking time: 30 minutes

1 Prepare the prawns while the rice is cooking.
2 Heat the oil in a frying pan. Add the onion and garlic and fry
   until the onion is golden brown.
3 Add the ground spices (coriander, roasted spices, red chilli,
   turmeric), the tomatoes, yoghurt, coconut and salt to the pan.
   Stir the mixture over the heat for two minutes.
4 Add the prawns and cook on medium heat until all the liquid has
   been absorbed and the oil appears on the surface of the
   mixture.
5 Do not stir too frequently or the prawns will become mushy.
   Remove the pan from the heat. Sprinkle over the garam
   masala, green chilli and chopped coriander leaves. Set the pan
   on one side while the rice is cooking.

Arrange the cooked rice and prawns in layers in a larger pan. Pour in
the milk and heat gently for three minutes to absorb the liquid. Tip
the contents from the cooking dish into the serving dish before
serving.

Serving Suggestions:
Serve hot with yoghurt, kerala (bitter gourd), aubergine, moong dal
and chapati.

Khatéwalé Kabuli Chunna
(Chickpeas with tamarind-North Indian Style)

Serves 4-6

This is a very popular dish from the Punjab, it is suitable to be served at parties and important ceremonies. You will find this dish to be of medium hotness.

Ingredients:	Metric	Imperial	American
Chickpeas, soaked overnight, cleaned and washed	*500 g*	*18 oz*	*18 oz*
Gram dal cleaned and washed	*50 g*	*2 oz*	*¼ cup*
Water	*2.8 l*	*5 pt*	*11 cups*
Bicarbonate of soda	*2.5 ml*	*½ tsp*	*½ tsp*
Salt to taste			
Oil or ghee	*75 ml*	*5 tbsp*	*5 tbsp*
Cumin seeds	*5 ml*	*1 tsp*	*1 tsp*
Large garlic cloves, crushed	*3*	*3*	*3*
Fresh ginger	*2.5 cm*	*1"*	*1"*
Large onion, finely chopped	*1*	*1*	*1*
Ground coriander	*10 ml*	*2 tsp*	*2 tsp*
Ground, roasted cumin	*5 ml*	*1 tsp*	*1 tsp*
Garam masala	*5 ml*	*1 tsp*	*1 tsp*
Ground turmeric	*2.5 ml*	*½ tsp*	*½ tsp*
Ground red chilli	*2.5 ml*	*½ tsp*	*½ tsp*
Tomatoes, tinned	*400 g*	*14 oz*	*2 cups*
Tamarind, soaked overnight and extract pulp	*50 g*	*2 oz*	*2 oz*

To garnish:

Green coriander leaves, chopped	*30 ml*	*2 tbsp*	*2 tbsp*
Small green chilli, chopped	*1*	*1*	*1*
Garam masala	*2.5 ml*	*1 tsp*	*1 tsp*

Khatéwalé Kabuli Chunna
(Chickpeas with tamarind-North Indian Style)

Cooking time: 1hr 40 minutes

1 Place the chickpeas, gram dal, bicarbonate of soda, salt and water in a large pan. If you do not have a pan large enough, add water gradually. Bring to the boil, skim off any scum and simmer over medium heat for 1 hr 20 minutes until the chickpeas are tender. Drain or absorb some of the liquid over the heat.
2 Meanwhile, heat the oil in a heavy based pan and fry the cumin seeds until lightly browned.
3 Add the garlic, ginger and onion and fry over medium heat until golden brown.
4 Stir in the ground spices and the tomatoes and cook until all the water has been absorbed and the oil appears on the top of the mixture.
5 Add the tamarind pulp and cook until all the liquid has been absorbed.
6 Stir in the cooked chickpeas and simmer over medium heat for a further 20 minutes until the mixture thickens.
7 Sprinkle over garnish ingredients.

Serving suggestion:

Serve hot with bhutoora or nan, tamarind chutney, dahibara, matar-paneer, potato curry, and salad (finely chopped onion, cucumber and tomato).

Bhutoora

Makes: 20

Bhutoora is one of the special and original breads of Punjab.
The appetite increases when one sees the bhutoora swelling like
a balloon while they are being fried!

Ingredients:	Metric	Imperial	American
Yeast, dried	*5 ml*	*1 tsp*	*1 tsp*
Sugar	*5 ml*	*1 tsp*	*1 tsp*
Water, tepid	*30 ml*	*2 tbsp*	*2 tbsp*

Place the above ingredients in a small bowl. Mix with a fork, cover
and leave in a warm place for 30 minutes. It should rise and foam
up.

Ingredients:	Metric	Imperial	American
Plain flour, sifted	*500 g*	*1 lb 2 oz*	*18 oz*
Margarine	*25 g*	*1 oz*	*1 oz*
Natural Yogurt	*100 g*	*4 oz*	*¹/₂ cup*
Salt	*large pinch*	*¹/₈ tsp*	*¹/₈ tsp*
Water, tepid	*100 ml*	*3 ¹/₂ fl oz*	*6 ¹/₂ tbsp*
Oil to fry			

1 Rub the margarine into the flour
2 Add the yogurt, salt and the risen yeast and mix thoroughly.
3 Knead the dough with warm water for about 5 minutes or until
  the dough is springy and satiny.
4 Cover and leave in a warm place for 3-4 hours or until the dough
  has risen to double its original size.

Cooking time: 30 minutes

1 Divide the dough into about 20 equal portions.
2 Take a portion of dough and roll into a ball.
3 Traditionally, put a little oil on the palm of your hands and flatten
  the ball, turning quickly from one palm to the other, until it is

Bhutoora

5 mm/¼ " thin (some people like it even thinner) or roll it out like puri with a rolling pin.

4 Heat the oil in a deep frying pan on high heat.

5 Slip the bhutoora into the hot oil from the edge of the pan.

6 Gently press the bhutoora with a slotted spoon all over and it will rise like a balloon

7 Fry both sides light brown.

I roll another bhutoora while one is frying.

Serving suggestion:

Serve with khatéwalé kabuli chunna, dahibara, matar-paneer, cauliflower or stuffed aubergine. The bhutooras can be reheated under the grill.

DAY
5

This is only the fifth day but
I am going to throw you in at the deep
end. Hard work, yes, but by the end of
this day's learning you'll be able to
hold
a grand party or a banquet
with great pride. I am sure
that you'll charm your friends with
your cullinary expertise. Stuffed
Murgh Musallum is
a wedding-party dish.

Today you can also learn how
to make Nan bread, this is my own
personal style. Lassi is a yoghurt drink
also very popular all over India. It is a
speciality of Punjab.

Stuffed Murgh Musallum
(Whole chicken with nuts, minced lamb and rice)

Serves: 4-6

Stuffed Murgh Musallum is one of the royal chicken dishes which is very nourishing, attractive and tasty. The dish is hot.

Ingredients:	Metric	Imperial	American
Medium chicken	1	1	1
Eggs	6	6	6

Skin, wash and prick the chicken all over with a fork. Hard boil the eggs and cut into halves lengthwise.

Preparing the Marinade:

	Metric	Imperial	American
Large garlic cloves	6	6	6
Fresh ginger	4 cm	1 1/2 "	1 1/2 "
Dried figs	2	2	2
Small green chilli (optional)	1	1	1
Lemon juice	30 ml	2 tbsp	2 tbsp
Sugar	10 ml	2 tsp	2 tsp
Garam masala	10 ml	2 tsp	2 tsp
Ground coriander	10 ml	2 tsp	2 tsp
Ground red chilli	2.5 ml	1/2 tsp	1/2 tsp
Ground turmeric	2.5 ml	1/2 tsp	1/2 tsp
Ground black pepper	1.25 ml	1/4 tsp	1/4 tsp
Roasted cumin	5 ml	1 tsp	1 tsp
Salt to taste			
Natural yoghurt	150 ml	1/4 pt	2/3 cup

Combine the last four ingredients (garlic, onion, ginger and water) in a blender and blend to make a smooth paste. Rub the paste all over the chicken and marinate for 3 hours.

Preparing the Filling:

Ingredients:	Metric	Imperial	American
Ghee	60 ml	4 tbsp	4 tbsp
Medium onion, thinly sliced	1	1	1
Minced lamb or mutton	200 g	7 oz	1 cup

Stuffed Murgh Musallum
(Whole chicken with nuts, minced lamb and rice)

DAY 5

Ingredients:	Metric	Imperial	American
Rice (Basmati or Patna), cleaned washed and drained	150 g	5 oz	²/₃ cup
Peas	200 g	7 oz	1 cup
Raisins	100 g	4 oz	¹/₄ cup
Almonds, blanched and cut in half lengthwise	50 g	2 oz	¹/₄ cup
Cashewnuts, cut in halves lengthwise	50 g	2 oz	¹/₄ cup
Pistachios	25 g	1 oz	1 oz
Fresh dill or	15 ml	1 tbsp	1 tbsp
Dried dill	7.5 ml	¹/₂ tbsp	¹/₂ tbsp
Saffron	2.5 ml	¹/₂ tsp	¹/₂ tsp
Ground corriander	10 ml	2 tsp	2 tsp
Garam masala	10 ml	2 tsp	2 tsp
Aniseed	5 ml	1 tsp	1 tsp
Ground red chilli	2.5 ml	¹/₂ tsp	¹/₂ tsp
Ground turmeric	2.5 ml	¹/₂ tsp	¹/₂ tsp
Salt to taste			
Water	300 ml	10 fl oz	1 ¹/₄ cups

Cooking time: 45 minutes

1 For best roasting effect place the marinated chicken on skewers or on a rack wire, sprinkle over 10 ml/2 tsp oil and place in a pre-heated oven on 200° C, 400° F or Gas mark 6 and roast for 45 minutes. Turn the chicken over 2 or 3 times and baste with the marinade.
2 Prepare the rice while the chicken is roasting.
3 Heat the ghee in a large heavy bottomed saucepan, on medium heat and fry the onions gently until golden brown.
4 Add the minced lamb and fry for 3 minutes.
5 Put in the rice and fry for a further 2 minutes.
6 Mix in the raisins, almonds, cashewnuts, pistachios, peas, saffron, dill, coriander, garam masala, aniseed, red chilli, turmeric, salt and water.

Stuffed Murgh Musallum
(Whole chicken with nuts, minced lamb and rice)

DAY 5

7 Bring to the boil, reduce the heat to low, close the lid and cook for 10 minutes or until the meat and the rice is tender and all the water has absorbed. Turn the heat off.

8 Stuff the chicken tightly with the filling mixture.

9 Prepare the sauce while the filling is cooking. (It can be prepared the day before.)

Sauce:

Ingredients:	Metric	Imperial	American
Oil	150 ml	10 tbsp	2/3 cup
Cumin	5 ml	1 tsp	1 tsp
Medium onion, coarsely chopped	1	1	1
*Cloves	6	6	6
*Peppercorns	6	6	6
Bay leaves	2	2	2
*Cardamom	2	2	2
*Cinnamon stick	2.5 cm	1"	1"
Large garlic cloves	5	5	5
Medium onion, coarsely chopped	3	3	3
Fresh ginger	2.5 cm	1"	1"
Water	45 ml	3 tbsp	3 tbsp

Combine the last four ingredients (garlic, onion, ginger and water) in a blender and blend to make a smooth paste (you do not require water if you are using a food processor).

Ingredients:	Metric	Imperial	American
Ground almond	15 ml	1 tbsp	1 tbsp
Ground coriander	15 ml	1 tbsp	1 tbsp
Groound roasted cumin	10 ml	2 tsp	2 tsp
Ground red chilli	2.5 ml	1/2 tsp	1/2 tsp
Canned tomatoes	400 g	14 oz	2 cups
Salt to taste			
Lemon juice	30 ml	2 tbsp	2 tbsp

Stuffed Murgh Musallum
(Whole chicken with nuts, minced lamb and rice)

To garnish:

Garam masala	5 ml	1 tsp	1 tsp

Ingredients:	**Metric**	**Imperial**	**American**
Green coriander leaves, chopped	30 ml	2 tbsp	2 tbsp
Small green chilli, chopped	1	1	1

Cooking time: 30 minutes

1 Heat the oil in a large heavy-bottomed saucepan on medium heat and brown the cumin seeds. Add the chopped onion, bay leaves, cloves, peppercorns, black cardamoms and cinnamon stick, and fry gently the chopped onions and the whole spices until golden brown.

2 Put in the blended paste and fry for a further few minutes until golden brown.

3 Stir in the almonds, coriander, roasted cumin, red chilli, salt and the tomatoes and cook until all the liquid has been absorbed.

4 Mix in the lemon juice and cook again until all the liquid is evaporated and the oil appears on the surface of the mixture.

5 Pour in 200 ml/ 7 fl oz water. Bring to the boil. Place the stuffed chicken in the sauce and baste the chicken with the sauce for a further 10 minutes on a medium-low heat (gently turn over twice) or until all the water has been absorbed.

Garnish Suggestion:

Place the cooked chicken on a large flat serving dish.

1 Arrange the left-over fillings around it. Place the egg pieces on top.

2 Sprinkle over the garnish before serving.

DAY 5

Roghni Nan

Makes: 12

In India people cook the nan bread in a tandoor. If one isn't available it can be baked in an oven.

Ingredients:	Metric	Imperial	American
Yeast, dried	10 ml	2 tsp	2 tsp
Sugar	10 ml	2 tsp	2 tsp
Water (tepid)	30 ml	2 tbsp	2 tbsp

Place the above ingredients in a small bowl. Mix with a fork, cover and leave in a warm place for 30 minutes. It should rise and foam up.

Plain flour, sifted	500 g	1 lb 2 oz	18 oz
Margarine or ghee	50 g	2 oz	$^1/_4$ cup
Bicarbonate of soda	1.5 ml	$^1/_4$ tsp	$^1/_4$ tsp
Salt	large pinch	$^1/_8$ tsp	$^1/_8$ tsp
Milk	125 ml	4 fl oz	$^1/_2$ cup
Yogurt	30 ml	2 tbsp	2 tbsp

1 Rub the margarine and the bicarbonate of soda into the flour.
2 Add the salt, yoghurt and the risen yeast and mix thoroughly.
3 Knead the dough with warm milk for 5 minutes or until the dough is springy and satiny.
4 Cover and leave in a warm place, for 3-4 hours or until the dough has risen to double the original size.

To sprinkle:

Milk to brush	15 ml	1 tbsp	1 tbsp
Sesame seeds	15 ml	1 tbsp	1 tbsp
Onion seeds	15 ml	1 tbsp	1 tbsp

Cooking Time: 9 minutes

1 Heat an oven to gas mark 9 (475° F, 240° C).
2 Roll half of the dough into a 15 cm/ 6" long strip. Divide it into 6 equal portions. Repeat with the rest of the dough.

Roghni Nan

3 Take a portion and flatten it with your palm into an oval shape about 5 mm/ ¼ " thick.
4 Place four or five nans onto a greased baking tray. Brush the tops with milk and sprinkle over the sesame and the onion seeds. Repeat with the rest of the nan.
5 Bake for seven minutes then reverse the position of the trays and bake for a further 2 minutes or until golden brown.

Serving suggestion:
Serve hot with all the tandoori dishes and Khatéwalé Kabuli Chunna.

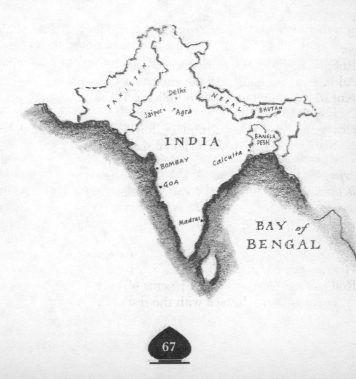

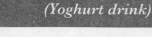

Lassi
(Yoghurt drink)

Makes: 6 glasses

This refreshing cool drink is enjoyed during the summer at breakfast (instead of tea) and at lunch time (instead of water) in India. It can be sweet or salty.

Ingredients:	Metric	Imperial	American
Natural yoghurt	*450 g*	*1 lb*	*16 oz*
Sugar	*60 g*	*4 tbsp*	*4 tbsp*
Water, cold	*100 ml*	*3.5 fl oz*	*½ cup*
Ice cubes (quantity depends upon weather)	*12*	*12*	*12*

Preparation time: 5 minutes

1 Combine the yoghurt and the sugar in a blender and blend for 2 minutes or until smooth.
2 Add the water and the ice cubes and blend for a further 1 minute or until a lot of foam appears (be careful not to blend for too long otherwise you may get butter and whey from the yoghurt!)

Serving suggestion:

Drink sweetened at breakfast with paratha / pudha / pakora / puri-aloo. For other meals especially during lunch Indians drink salty lassi because, due to the heat, they lose a lot of salt in perspiration. To make salty lassi use the same recipe except add salt, 5 ml/1 tsp ground roasted cumin, 1.5 ml/¼ tsp black pepper and 100 ml/ 3.5 fl oz/ ½ cup extra water to the yoghurt.

DAY
6

Today you can increase your repertoire of sweets, chutney and snacks/starters. My mother's style of stuffed bread rolls are admired by everyone - young and old alike. My son Sumeet is very fond of Gulab Jamun which are rich in protein and carbohydrate.

Stuffed breadroll has a lovely tangy, spicy mixture of potato, peas, onions and raisins.

Stuffed Bread Rolls

Makes: 18

Bread rolls are an extremely tasty, nourishing and filling snack/starter. You will find the recipe to be of medium hotness.

Ingredients:	Metric	Imperial	American
Potatoes, boiled in jackets, peeled and mashed	500 g	1 lb 2 oz	18 oz
Frozen peas, thawed or	250 g	9 oz	9 oz
Fresh peas - cook in water until tender	250 g	9 oz	9 oz
Medium onion, finely chopped	1	1	1
Small green chilli, chopped	1	1	1
Raisins	100 g	4 oz	½ cup
Lemon juice	30 ml	2 tbsp	2 tbsp
Green coriander leaves, chopped	30 ml	2 tbsp	2 tbsp
Garam masala	5 ml	1 tsp	1 tsp
Ground red chilli	2.5 ml	½ tsp	½ tsp
Salt to taste			

1 Place the mashed potatoes, peas, onions, green chilli, raisins, lemon, coriander leaves and the garam masala, red chilli and salt into a large bowl and mix them well.
2 Divide them into 18 equal portions. Roll them round and give them an oblong shape. Set them to one side.

Bread, white thin sliced, cut them in halves	9	9	9
Oil to fry			

Cooking Time: 30 minutes

1 Fill a saucepan with warm water. Put a half slice of bread in it and soak for about 10-15 seconds.

Stuffed Bread Rolls

2 Take out the soaked bread (put another piece of bread in the water) and place onto the left palm of your hand. Press it gently with your right hand palm and squeeze out all the water.

3 Place one portion of potato mixture onto the squeezed bread. Gently roll the bread around the mixture. Keep pressing the edges so that the filling won't come out. Make more while the oil is heating.

4 Heat the oil in a deep frying pan on medium heat. Fry three or four stuffed bread rolls together until they are golden brown. I stuff the bread pieces for the next batch while one is frying.

Serving suggestion:

Serve hot at tea with chutney, gulab jamun and barfi or at meal as a starter.

Gulab Jamun

Makes: 30

The gulab jamun is a delicious and popular sweet of India. It is served at almost all parties and special occasions.

Ingredients:	Metric	Imperial	American
Full cream milk powder	100 g	4 oz	1 cup
Ghee, melted	30 ml	2 tbsp	2 tbsp
Plain white flour	15 ml	1 tbsp	1 tbsp
Semolina	15 ml	1 tbsp	1 tbsp
Bicarbonate of soda	small pinch	small pinch	small pinch
Milk, tepid	105 ml	7 tbsp	7 tbsp

Place the milk powder, ghee, flour, semolina and bicarbonate of soda in a bowl and mix thoroughly. Pour in the milk and make a soft dough. Cover and leave for 20 minutes.

Filling:

Sultanas	15 g	1/2 oz	1/2 oz
Almonds, blanched and finely chopped	6	6	6
Pistachioes, finely chopped	5	5	5
Ground green cardamoms	2.5 ml	1/2 tsp	1/2 tsp

Syrup

Sugar	250 g	9 oz	9 oz
Water	200 ml	7 fl oz	1 cup
Ghee and oil to fry (equal quantities)			

Cooking Time: 30 minutes

1 Heat the ghee and oil (mixture) in a deep frying pan on medium low heat.
2 While the fat is heating divide the dough into 20 equal parts and roll into small balls.
3 Flatten each one, place on a little filling and roll them round again.

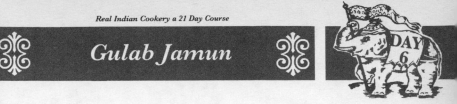

Gulab Jamun

4 Add 10 balls to the frying pan and gently fry until golden brown. Keep on turning them over (don't fry them too quickly otherwise they will not be cooked inside. If the fat is too hot reduce the heat to low). Take them out with a slotted spoon and place them on a cooling tray. Repeat until all of them are fried.

5 While you are frying the gulab jamun, place the sugar and water in a saucepan to boil on medium heat. Turn the heat off as soon as the sugar has dissolved.

6 Add the fried gulab jamun to the syrup. Bring them to the boil again on medium heat, then reduce to a low heat and cook for a further 5 minutes.

Serving suggestion:

Serve hot or cold after the meal and at tea time with samosa, pakora or breadroll.

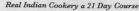

Dhaniya Chutney

Fills: 450 g/ 1 lb Jam jar

This chutney has an exquisite and individual flavour. It is a hot recipe.

Ingredients:	Metric	Imperial	American
Bunch of coriander leaves, washed and coarsely cut the leaves and the tender stems	1	1	1
Medium onion, coarsely chopped	1	1	1
Small green chilli	1	1	1
Large lemon, extract juice	1	1	1
Ground red chilli	2.5 ml	¹/₂ tsp	¹/₂ tsp
Garam masala	2.5 ml	¹/₂ tsp	¹/₂ tsp
Water	30 ml	2 tbsp	2 tbsp
Salt to taste			

Preparation time: 20 minutes

Combine all the ingredients in a blender and blend to make a fine paste.

Serving suggestion:

Serve it at meals and at tea with samosa, breadrolls, pakora, kabab and mathi etc. The dhaniya chutney will keep about one week in a clean, airtight jar or container in a fridge.

DAY
7

Today you will learn to make Pork Vindaloo. The pork can also be substituted for lamb or chicken. Moong ki Hari Dal (whole green mung beans) is cooked in a Punjabi style. The texture should neither be too thick nor too runny.

Kulfi is one of my favourite ice creams. When I came to this country I did not have time to prepare Kulfi the traditional way therefore I tried different combinations of cream without much success. Fifteen years ago I found this combination of alternative to real cream and evaporated milk produced exactly the right textured mixture. Falooda is an optional garnish for Kulfi. It can also be used as a drink.

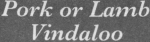

Pork or Lamb Vindaloo

Serves: 4-6

In this dish I have specially roasted the ingredients to obtain a dark colour and the finest possible flavour. The dish would be suitable for a party meal and is very hot.

Ingredients:	Metric	Imperial	American
Pork or lamb, cut into 5 cm/ 2" pieces, fat trimmed off and washed	500 g	1 lb 2 oz	18 oz
Whole coriander, cleaned	15 ml	1 tbsp	1 tbsp
Cumin seeds	10 ml	2 tsp	2 tsp
Mustard seeds	10 ml	2 tsp	2 tsp
Peppercorns	5	5	5
Cloves	5	5	5
Small dried red chilli, break into a few pieces	4	4	4
Cinnamon	2.5 cm	1"	1"
Black cardamom, only use seeds	1	1	1

Heat a flat frying pan on medium heat and roast all the spices until brown. Grind them in a grinder to a fine powder.

	Metric	Imperial	American
Turmeric	2.5 ml	½ tsp	½ tsp
Salt to taste			

Mix the turmeric and salt in the roasted powder.

Ingredients:	Metric	Imperial	American
Large garlic cloves, chopped	5	5	5
Fresh ginger, chopped	4 cm	1½"	1½"
Vinegar	60 ml	4 tbsp	4 tbsp

Combine all the chopped and roasted ingredients in a blender and blend to make a smooth paste. Rub the paste into the meat pieces and leave to marinate overnight.

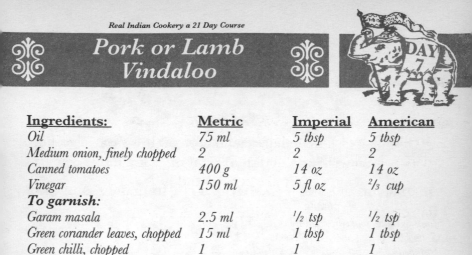

Pork or Lamb Vindaloo

DAY 7

Ingredients:	Metric	Imperial	American
Oil	75 ml	5 tbsp	5 tbsp
Medium onion, finely chopped	2	2	2
Canned tomatoes	400 g	14 oz	14 oz
Vinegar	150 ml	5 fl oz	⅔ cup
To garnish:			
Garam masala	2.5 ml	½ tsp	½ tsp
Green coriander leaves, chopped	15 ml	1 tbsp	1 tbsp
Green chilli, chopped	1	1	1

Cooking time: 1 hour 10 minutes

1 Heat the oil in a large heavy-bottomed saucepan on medium heat and gently fry the onion until golden brown.
2 Add the marinated pieces and fry for a further 15 minutes or until golden brown.
3 Stir in the tomatoes and fry until all the liquid has been absorbed and the oil appears on the surface of the mixture.
4 Put in the vinegar and 250 ml/ 9 fl oz/ 1 cup water. Bring to the boil. Close the lid, reduce the heat to medium-low and cook for 40 minutes or until the meat is tender.
5 Sprinkle over the garnish before serving.

Serving suggestion:
Serve hot with rice, chapati, rayta and a bean-potato or an okra dish.

Sabat Moong Ki Hari Dal
(Whole Green Mung Beans- North Indian style)

DAY 7

Serves: 4-6

This dal is rich in both taste and protein. It is easily digested.
You will find this dish to be of medium hotness.

Ingredients:	Metric	Imperial	American
Whole, green mung beans, washed and soaked for an hour	250 g	9 oz	1 cup
Water	1.5 l	3 pt	6 cups
Turmeric	large pinch	1/8 tsp	1/8 tsp
Salt to taste			

Tarka

Oil or ghee	45 ml	4 tbsp	4 tbsp
Medium onion, finely chopped	1	1	1
Fresh ginger, finely chopped	1 cm	1/2 "	1/2 "
Mustard seeds	5 ml	1 tsp	1 tsp
Cumin seeds	5 ml	1 tsp	1 tsp
Garam masala	5 ml	1 tsp	1 tsp
Ground red chilli	2.5 ml	1/2 tsp	1/2 tsp
Ground turmeric	large pinch	large pinch	large pinch
Tomatoes, tinned	400 g	14 oz	2 cups

To garnish:

Green corriander leaves, chopped	15 ml	1 tbsp	1 tbsp
Garam masala	2.5 ml	1/2 tsp	1/2 tsp
Small green chilli, chopped	1	1	1

Cooking time: 1 hour

1 Place the dal, turmeric, salt and the water in a large saucepan.
   Bring to the boil, skim off any scum and simmer for 50 minutes
   on medium heat, until tender.
2 While the dal is cooking prepare the tarka. Heat the ghee in a
   heavy bottomed saucepan. Add the mustard seeds, when they

Sabat Moong Ki Hari Dal
(Whole Green Mung Beans-
North Indian style)

DAY 7

start cracking add the cumin seeds, then the onion, ginger and fry until golden brown.

3 Add the turmeric, red chilli, garam masala and the tomatoes. Fry until all the water has been absorbed and the ghee apears on the top of the mixture.

4 Stir in the cooked dal and simmer for a further ten minutes.

5 Sprinkle over the garnish before serving.

Serving sugggestion:

Serve hot with rice, chapati, matar-paneer, cauliflower, yoghurt and a meat dish.

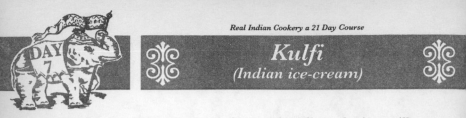

Kulfi
(Indian ice-cream)

Kulfi is traditionally made by continually reducing milk. However this is a long and tedious process. I have finally found the perfect combination of creams which can produce the same - if not better effect. It is also much quicker!

Ingredients:	Metric	Imperial	American
Alternate to real cream			
(non-dairy cream made with			
vegetable oil)	*284 ml*	*10 fl oz*	*1 1/4 cups*
Evaporated milk	*410 g*	*14 1/2 fl oz*	*2 cups*
Sugar or to taste	*60 ml*	*4 tbsp*	*4 tbsp*
Almonds, blanched and thinly			
sliced	*40 g*	*1 1/2 oz*	*1 1/2 oz*
Pistachioes, thinly sliced	*15 g*	*1/2 oz*	*1/2 oz*
Essence: rose or kevera water	*10 ml*	*2 tsp*	*2 tsp*
Ground green cardamon	*5 ml*	*1 tsp*	*1 tsp*

1 Whisk the cream, evaporated milk and the sugar until (very) thick.
2 Add all the ingredients and mix thoroughly.
3 Mix and pour into kulfi containers (conical shaped), or small plastic cups with lids or empty ice-cream containers can be used instead.
4 Cover and freeze. (Stir kulfi every 20-30 minutes to prevent the nuts settling at the bottom.)

Serving suggestion:
Cut kulfi into small rounds and serve cold (with falooda) after a meal.

Falooda

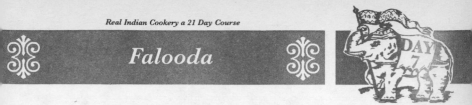

Makes: 4 glasses

Falooda is used to garnish kulfi (Indian ice-cream) and is consumed as a cold drink especially during the summer. When used as a drink food colours and lots of crushed ice are added.

Ingredients:	Metric	Imperial	American
Cornflour	50 g	2 oz	¼ cup
Water	250 ml	9 fl oz	1 cup
Sev machine (vermichelli machine)			
Syrup:			
Sugar	25 g	1 oz	2 tbsp
Water	50 ml	2 fl oz	¼ cup
Essence: rose or kevera water	5 ml	1 tsp	1 tsp
Food colour, yellow, red or green	1.5 ml	¼ tsp	¼ tsp

Place the water and the sugar on medium heat. Bring to the boil and simmer until the sugar is dissolved. Add the colour and essence when cold.

Ingredients: *Crushed ice*

Cooking time: 2 minutes

1 Keep iced cold water ready in a bowl. Place a colander on it.
2 Mix the cornflour and the water in a saucepan. Place it on medium heat, stirring constantly. When the mixture is thick and becomes transparent and slightly yellowish remove from heat.
3 Fill the sev machine with the cooked paste. Turn the machine handle swiftly over the seive in the iced cold water bowl and let the long strands fall on it.
4 Repeat until you have used all the paste.
5 Leave the falooda to set for 1 hour.
6 Lift your colander out and drain out all the water.
7 Add chilled falooda to the syrup.

Serving suggestion:

Half fill the glasses with the crushed ice. Then fill them with falooda. Pour over the cold syrup and eat it with a spoon. Also one can garnish one's kulfi by putting falooda over it.

The South Indian bread Dosa with coconut chutney is very popular among all parts of India. It charmed my daughter Sajni even when she was only three years old! She said "Mummy, this is the yummiest meal I have ever eaten in my whole life!"

Fried fish compliments vegetable pulao. Vegetable pulao with cashewnuts, raisins, peas and long strands of carrrot is a delight for both vegetarians and non vegetarians. If in a rush it can be eaten with plain yoghurt for a meal.

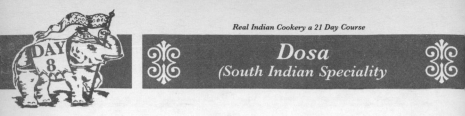

Dosa
(South Indian Speciality

Makes: 12

Dosa is one of the most popular and best breads from Southern India. You will find the dish to be of medium hotness.

Preparing the dosa mixture:

Ingredients:	Metric	Imperial	American
Rice, soaked overnight (or for two hours in luke warm water) and blended in a liquidiser with water until smooth	75 ml	2.5 fl oz	⅓ cup
Urud ki dhuli dal, soaked overnight (or for two hours in luke warm water) and blended with water until smooth	75 ml	2.5 fl oz	⅓ cup

1 Mix the liquidised rice and dal and whip for five minutes.
2 Cover and leave in a warm place to rise for 24 hours.

Preparing the filling:

	Metric	Imperial	American
Potatoes, boiled in jackets, peeled and cut into small pieces about 5 mm/¼"	1 kg	2 lb 4 oz	36 oz
Oil	75 ml	5 tbsp	5 tbsp
Mustard seeds	5 ml	1 tsp	1 tsp
Cumin seds	5 ml	1 tsp	1 tsp
Garam masala	10 ml	2 tsp	2 tsp
Ground coriander	5 ml	1 tsp	1 tsp
Ground roasted cumin	5 ml	1 tsp	1 tsp
Ground ginger	2.5 ml	½ tsp	½ tsp
Ground red chilli	2.5 ml	½ tsp	½ tsp
Ground turmeric	2.5 ml	½ tsp	½ tsp
Salt to taste			

Tomatoes, tinned	400 g	14 oz	2 cups
Lemon juice	60 ml	4 tbsp	4 tbsp
Coriander leaves, chopped	60 ml	4 tbsp	4 tbsp
Small green chilli, chopped	1	1	1
Oil to fry			

Cooking time: 20 minutes

1 Heat the oil in a large heavy bottomed saucepan on medium heat. Add the mustard seeds and when they start crackling brown the cumin seeds (this will happen in a matter of seconds).
2 Put in the potato pieces and fry for 10 minutes or until light brown.
3 Stir in the ground spices (garam masala, coriander, roasted cumin, ginger, red chilli, turmeric) salt and then the tomatoes and cook until all the liquid has been absorbed.
4 Pour in 200 ml/ 7 fl oz/ 1 cup water. Bring to the boil.
Reduce the heat to medium-low and simmer for 3 minutes. Mix in the green coriander, green chilli and the lemon juice.

Preparing the dosa:
Frying time: 40 minutes

1 Place a flat frying pan on medium low heat. While the pan is heating whip the dosa mixture for 2 minutes, and add a large pinch of salt and 50 ml/ 3 $^{1}/_{3}$ tbsp water to make a smooth batter.
2 Smear the frying pan with 5 ml/ 1 tsp oil. Pour on about 45 ml/ 3 tbsp batter and immediately lift the pan up and turn around to spread the batter into a thin circle.
3 Cook for two minutes (the edges will begin to leave the pan). Then pour 10 ml/ 2 tsp oil around the edges. Turn the dosa over with a flat spoon and pour 10 ml/ 2 tsp oil as before. Cook both sides light golden brown.
4 Place the dosa on a plate, put 30 ml/ 2 tbsp (or more) hot filling on half the circle and fold over the other half (giving a half moon shape).
5 Continue making dosas till the mixture finishes - one does not need to initially smear the pan for the second dosa.

Serving suggestion:
Serve hot with coconut chutney and sambar.

Coconut Chutney
(South Indian Style)

Makes: 1 lb jar

This cooling refreshing chutney is popular all over India. The mixture of yoghurt, coconut, mint, coriander leaves and lentil produce a unique taste. The recipe is hot.

Ingredients:	Metric	Imperial	American
Yoghurt	150 g	5 oz	2/3 cup
Coconut desiccated (or fresh grated)	75 g	3 oz	1/3 cup
Lemon juice	60 ml	4 tbsp	4 tbsp
Green coriander leaves only	30 ml	2 tbsp	2 tbsp
Mint leaves only	15 ml	1 tbsp	1 tbsp
Gram dal, soaked in warm water for 4 hours	15 ml	1 tbsp	1 tbsp
Ground roasted cumin	5 ml	1 tsp	1 tsp
Ground red chilli	2.5 ml	1/2 tsp	1/2 tsp
Fresh ginger, coarsely chopped	5 ml	1/4 "	1/4 "
Small green chilli	1	1	1
Salt to taste			

Combine all the above ingredients in a blender and blend to make a smooth paste. Place in a bowl.

Tarka

	Metric	Imperial	American
Oil	15 ml	1 tbsp	1 tbsp
Asafoetida	large pinch	1/8 tsp	1/8 tsp
Mustard seeds	2.5 ml	1/2 tsp	1/2 tsp
Urud ki dhuli dal, soaked in warm water for 1 hour	5 ml	1 tsp	1 tsp

Coconut Chutney
(South Indian Style)

DAY
8

Cooking time: 2 minutes

1 Heat the oil in a small saucepan on medium heat. Add the asafoetida and the mustard seeds. When the mustard seeds start crackling fry the urud dal until light brown.
2 Pour this over the ground chutney and mix.

Serving suggestion:
Serve with dosa, sambar and idli.

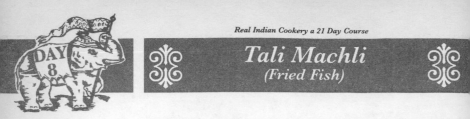

Tali Machli
(Fried Fish)

Serves: 4-6

This dish is very popular in the east and on the south coast of India. The piquant spicy flavour of the paste contrasts well with the delicate flavour of the fish. The dish is of medium hotness.

Ingredients:	Metric	Imperial	American
Fish, cod fillets, skinned, cut into			
5 cm / 2" pieces, washed and			
pat dried	500 g	1 lb 2 oz	18 oz
Large garlic cloves	5	5	5
Medium onion, coarsely chopped	2	2	2
Fresh ginger	2.5 cm	1"	1"
Small green chilli	1	1	1
Vinegar	100 ml	3.5 fl oz	1/2 cup
*Dried pomegranate seeds	5 ml	1 tsp	1 tsp
(optional)			

Combine all the above ingredients except the fish in a blender and blend to make a smooth paste.

Garam masala	5 ml	1 tsp	1 tsp
Ground roasted cumin	5 ml	1 tsp	1 tsp
Tymol seeds (ajwain), cleaned	5 ml	1 tsp	1 tsp
Ground red chilli	2.5 ml	1/2 tsp	1/2 tsp
Salt to taste			

1 Place the blended paste, ground spices (garam masala, roasted cumin, red chilli) salt and the tymol seeds in a large flat dish and mix them well.
2 Add the fish pieces and rub the paste on them thoroughly.
3 Cover and leave them to marinate for 2 hours.

Ingredients: *Oil to fry*

Tali Machli
(Fried Fish)

DAY 8

Cooking time: 1 hour

1 Remove the fish pieces from the marinade and set them on one side.
2 Place the marinade in a saucepan and dry off the liquid on medium heat (it will take about 30 minutes).
3 Coat the fish pieces evenly with the reduced marinade.
4 Heat a flat frying pan on medium low heat. Pour 60 ml/ 4 tbsp oil in the pan. Place in 4-5 fish pieces and fry gently till golden brown on all sides, taking care not to break them. Turn them over only 2-3 times.

Serving suggestion:

Serve hot with vegetable pulao, dal and a potato-bean dish at a meal or at tea with chutney, rasgula and barfi.

Vegetable Pulao with Nuts

Serves: 4-6

This dish is a treasure for vegetarians. The combination of nuts, spices and vegetables give it a very distinctive flavour. I always prepare it for a party. (This dish is not hot.)

Ingredients:	Metric	Imperial	American
Rice (patna or basmati), cleaned washed and drained	250 g	9 oz	1 cup
Ghee	90 ml	6 tbsp	6 tbsp
Cumin seeds	5 ml	1 tsp	1 tsp
Cloves	5	5	5
Peppercorns	5	5	5
Bay leaves	2	2	2
Cinnamon stick	2.5 cm	1"	1"
Black cardamom	1	1	1
Medium onion, thinly sliced	1	1	1
Garam masala	5 ml	1 tsp	1 tsp
Ground mace	1.5 ml	1/4 tsp	1/4 tsp
Ground nutmeg	1.5 ml	1/4 tsp	1/4 tsp
Salt to taste			
Peas frozen or fresh (shelled)	250 g	9 oz	1 cup
Carrots, peeled, washed and grated lengthwise	150 g	5 oz	5 oz
Rasins	75 g	3 oz	1/2 cup
Cashewnuts, cut in halves lengthwise	50 g	2 oz	1/4 cup
Water	575 ml	20 fl oz	2 1/2 cups

Cooking time: 45 minutes

1 Heat the ghee in a large heavy bottomed saucepan and brown the cumin seeds. Add the sliced onion, the whole spices (bay leaves, cloves, peppercorns, black cardamons, cinnamon) and fry until golden brown.

Vegetable Pulao with Nuts

2 Mix in the drained rice and fry for 2 minutes.

3 Stir in the ground spices (garam masala, macc, nutmeg), salt and then the carrots, peas, raisins and nuts.

4 Pour in the water. Bring to the boil. Reduce heat to low. Close the lid and cook for 15 minutes. If there is any water left, dry off and cook on high heat (do not stir but tip the pan a little to check the water). Turn the heat off and leave for at least 5 minutes before serving.

Serving suggestion:
Serve hot with rayta, a vegetable kofta dish and whole cauliflower.

Optional garnish:

Ingredients:	Metric	Imperial	American
Potato, peeled, washed and cut like chips	250 g	9 oz	9 oz
Oil to fry			

Heat the oil in a deep frying pan, and fry the potato chips until crispy golden brown. Garnish the rice with hot chips.

DAY 9

Today is devoted towards another popular starter known in India as Pakora, but more commonly in the UK as Onion Bhaji. I have written the recipe for this book using a mixture of vegetables. They are very delicious.

Dalmod is known in the UK as Bombay mix. It is an excellent nibble with any kind of drink. Don't get disheartened if you haven't got a sev machine. Some members of my evening class improvised a sev machine with an icing bag and colander. It's not brilliant but good enough to start off with - later you can buy one from an Asian grocery shop.

Pakora (Onion and Spinach)

DAY 9

Serves: 4-6

Some Asian restaurants in the UK often sell the pakora by the name of onion bhaji which is a misuse of the name. It is one of the delicious snacks which is eaten in every part of India at tea time. One can make the pakoras with one vegetable or a mixture of vegetables.

Ingredients:	Metric	Imperial	American
Batter			
Gram flour, sifted	250 g	9 oz	9 oz
Green coriander leaves, chopped	30 ml	2 tbsp	2 tbsp
Oil	15 ml	1 tbsp	1 tbsp
Gram masala	5 ml	1 tsp	1 tsp
Ground red chilli	5 ml	1 tsp	1 tsp
Ground roasted cumin	5 ml	1 tsp	1 tsp
Tymol seeds (ajwain), cleaned	5 ml	1 tsp	1 tsp
Small green chilli, chopped	1	1	1
Salt to taste			
Water lukewarm	225 ml	8 fl oz	1 cup

Place the sifted flour in a bowl and rub the oil into the flour. Add all the above ingredients into the bowl. Gradually pour in the water to make a thick batter and set the bowl on one side while you cut the vegetables and onion.

Onion and vegetable mixture

Medium onion, thinly sliced	1	1	1
Fenugreek leaves (or dried 1 tbsp)	30 ml	2 tbsp	2 tbsp
Spinach, washed and chopped	30 ml	2 tbsp	2 tbsp
Medium potato, peeled and grated	1	1	1
Medium carrot, peeled and grated	1	1	1

Add the above onion and vegetable mixture into the batter.

Pakora
(Onion and Spinach)

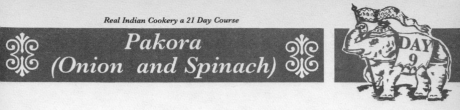

Cooking time: 25 minutes

1 Place the oil in a deep frying pan and heat it on medium heat. (If using vegetable pieces dip one by one into the batter and fry 7-8 pieces together).

2 Put 15 ml/ 1 tbsp mixture into the hot oil and fry 7 or 8 pakoras together.

3 When they are lightly brown from all sides keep on pressing and turning them over until they are cooked and golden brown on all sides.

Serving suggestion:

Serve hot at tea time with tamarind or dhaniya chutney, gulab jamun and barfi. If any pakoras are left over, I reheat them under the grill next day, wrap them in a slice of bread or chapati

Dalmod
(Bombay Mix)

and enjoy eating them with a cup of tea.

Makes: 1 medium tin

Dalmod is a beautiful combination of several nuts, lentil, rice flakes, sev etc. It is an excellent accompaniment for drinks. Dalmod is consumed not only for daily use, but is served during parties also.

Ingredients:	Metric	Imperial	American
Preparing the sev			
Gram flour, sifted	*150 g*	*5 oz*	*²/₃ cup*
Oil	*10 ml*	*2 tsp*	*2 tsp*
Garam masala	*2.5 ml*	*¹/₂ tsp*	*¹/₂ tsp*
Ground red chilli	*2.5 ml*	*¹/₂ tsp*	*¹/₂ tsp*
Tymol seeds	*2.5 ml*	*¹/₂ tsp*	*¹/₂ tsp*
Salt to taste			
Water, lukewarm	*100 ml*	*3¹/₂ fl oz*	*6¹/₂ tbsp*

Cooking time: 50 minutes

1 Place the sifted flour in a bowl.
2 Rub in the oil then mix the above spices thoroughly. Gradually pour in the water to make a smooth batter.

Oil to fry
Sev or vermicelli machine

3 Place the oil in a deep frying pan on medium heat. Place a small thread nozzle on the sev machine and fill to ³/₄ with the batter.
4 Hold the machine above the hot oil, slowly press the handle or turn it round (depending upon the type of machine you have), swiftly moving the hand holding the machine in a circle and let the batter fall in long strips – do not overlap the strips.
5 Fry until light golden brown. Remove with a slotted spoon and leave to cool. Break into 2.5 cm/ 1" pieces.

Preparing the Chevda:

Pawa (flaked rice)	*100 g*	*4 oz*	*1 cup*

Dalmod
(Bombay Mix)

Oil to fry

Heat the oil in a deep frying pan on high heat. Place a handful of pawa into the hot oil. Immediately turn them over and take them out (reduce the heat to low while taking them out, heat your oil again on high heat before frying more pawa).

Ingredients:	Metric	Imperial	American
Preparing the Chickpeas or Lentils:			
Chickpeas, cleaned, soaked overnight, washed and completely dry	*100 g*	*4 oz*	*1 cup*
Oil to fry			

Heat the oil in a deep frying pan on high heat. Fry the chickpeas until crispy and golden brown. Chickpeas tend to pop so do cover a little while frying.

Preparing the Kaju (cashewnuts):

Cashewnuts	*100 g*	*4 oz*	*1 cup*
Oil to fry			

Heat the oil in a deep frying pan on medium-low heat and fry the cashewnuts until light golden brown.

Preparing the Moongphali (peanuts):

Fresh shelled peanuts	*150 g*	*5 oz*	*²/₃ cup*
Oil to fry			

Heat the oil in a deep frying pan on medium heat and fry peanuts until crispy golden brown.

Raisins	*150 g*	*5 oz*	*³/₄ cup*

Tarka:

Oil	*15 ml*	*1 tbsp*	*1 tbsp*
Mustard seeds	*5 ml*	*1 tsp*	*1 tsp*
Garam masala	*5 ml*	*1 tsp*	*1 tsp*

Dalmod
(Bombay Mix)

Ground roasted cumin	5 ml	1 tsp	1 tsp
Ingredients:	**Metric**	**Imperial**	**American**
Aniseed	15 ml	1 tbsp	1 tbsp
Ground red chilli	2.5 ml	½ tsp	½ tsp
Salt to taste			
Sugar	15 ml	1 tbsp	1 tbsp
Citric acid	5 ml	1 tsp	1 tsp

1 Heat the oil in a large heavy bottomed saucepan. Add the mustard seeds when they start crackling stir in all the ground spices (garam masala, cumin, red chilli), salt and the raisins.

2 Turn the heat off. When slightly hot mix in the sugar and the citric acid. Add fried sev, chevda, chickpeas, kaju and moongphali in tarka. If the saucepan is not large enough place everything in a large bowl. Mix it thoroughly.

Preservation:

When cold keep it in an airtight container. It will keep over a fortnight.

Serving suggestion:

Serve at tea or as a nibble with drinks.

Balushahi

Makes: 12

Balushahi is a sweet snack. The members of my cookery classes called them doughnuts. One can keep them for a fortnight in an airtight container.

Ingredients:	Metric	Imperial	American
Plain flour, sifted	200 g	7 oz	1 cup
Margarine or ghee	50 g	2 oz	2 oz
Bicarbonate of soda	large pinch	1/8 tsp	1/8 tsp
Water, lukewarm	100 ml	3 1/2 fl oz	1/2 cup

1 Place the flour and the bicarbonate of soda in a bowl. Add the margarine and rub into the flour. Pour in the water and knead until the dough is soft, springy and satiny.

Ingredients:	Metric	Imperial	American
Sugar	150 g	5 oz	2/3 cup
Water	100 ml	3 1/2 fl oz	1/2 cup
Ground green cardamon	2.5 ml	1/2 tsp	1/2 tsp

Ghee and oil to fry (mix equal quantities)

Cooking Time: 1 hour

1 Heat the ghee and the oil in a deep frying pan on a medium heat. While the fat is heating divide the dough into 12 equal portions. Roll them into balls with the palm of your hands. Flatten them to about 1.2 cm/ 1/2" thick and press in the centre with your finger.

2 Slip the balushahies into the hot fat. Turn the heat off and leave them until the fat stops simmering.

3 Turn them over and heat them again on a medium heat. As soon as the fat starts boiling, turn the heat off. Repeat until the balushahies are risen and they are golden brown. Take them out with a slotted spoon and set them on one side.

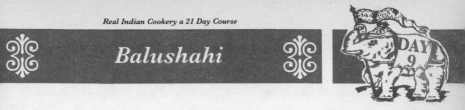

Balushahi

4 Place the sugar, cardamon and the water in a saucepan. Bring to the boil on a medium heat. As soon as the sugar is dissolved add the fried balushahis and let them simmer until the syrup is ready to set (test by dropping a drop of syrup into a cup of cold water, if the drop sets at the bottom, it is ready).

5 Turn the heat off. Keep on turning and coating the balushahi until they are well coated with syrup and are cold.

Serving suggestion:

Serve at tea with gulab jamun, pakora, samosa and chutney.

Today you will meet menus from both the South and the North of India. Onion Paratha is very quick and easy to make. Many Indians take this bread to school or work to give them a nourishing and filling lunch. Usually it is eaten with pickle/ plain natural yoghurt/ sabji (a vegetable dish e.g. okra, bitter gourd, cauliflower and potato) and urud dal. The method of cooking urud dal in this book is Punjabi style and this is one of my father's favourite dishes.

DAY 10

Onion Paratha (Bread)

Makes 12

Onion paratha is one of the simplest parathas to make and it is one of Indian children's packed lunch items. Chop the onion very finely otherwise it will be difficult to roll.

Ingredients:	Metric	Imperial	American
Brown chapati flour	525 g	1 lb 3 oz	19 oz
Medium onion, finely chopped	1	1	1
Small green chilli, finely chopped	1	1	1
Green coriander leaves, chopped	30 ml	2 tbsp	2 tbsp
Oil	15 ml	1 tbsp	1 tbsp
Garam masala	5 ml	1 tsp	1 tsp
Tymol seeds (ajwain)	5 ml	1 tsp	1 tsp
Ground red chilli	2.5 ml	½ tsp	½ tsp
Salt to taste			
Water, lukewarm	250 ml	9 fl oz	1 cup

Place all the above ingredients into a large bowl with 500 g/ 1 lb 2 oz/ 18 oz flour (keep the rest of the flour for rolling) and mix well. Pour in the water and make a soft dough. Knead it for 5 minutes or until the dough is springy and satiny. Cover and leave for 20 minutes.

Butter or ghee to smear
Oil to fry

Cooking time: 40 minutes

1 Heat a flat frying pan on a medium heat. While the frying pan is heating, divide the dough into 12 equal portions.
2 Take a portion of dough and roll it into a ball on the palm of your hands. Dust it with flour, flatten it and roll into a small circle. Smear half with 2.5 ml/ ½ tsp ghee or butter and fold it in half. Smear the half again with ghee and fold again (one should now have a triangle).

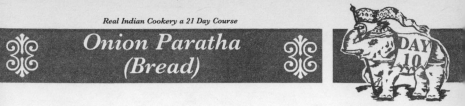

Onion Paratha (Bread)

3 Roll out again with the help of a little dry flour to 0.2 cm/ ⅛"
    thick (keeping the triangular shape).
4 Place the onion paratha on the hot frying pan and cook both sides
    dry like a chapati. Then pour 7.5 ml/ ½ tbsp oil over it, fry
    the first side until light brown. Make 6 or 7 small slits on the
    paratha. Pour another 7.5 ml/ ½ tbsp oil and fry the other side
    light golden brown as well.

Serving suggestion:

Serve hot with pickle, butter, natural yogurt, fried okra, urud
ki sukhi dal and undé ki bhaji.

DAY 10

Aloo, Gobhi and Gosht
(North Indian Style Potato, Cauliflower and Meat Curry)

Serves: 4-6

This is a lovely meat dish with vegetables. One can add a
vegetable according to one's taste.
This is a medium hot dish.

Ingredients:	Metric	Imperial	American
Meat, boned, cut into 2.5 cm/ 1" pieces, fat trimmed off and washed	500 g	1 lb 2 oz	18 oz
Cauliflower, cut into 2.5 cm/ 1" florets	250 g	9 oz	9 oz
Potato peeled, cut into 2.5 cm/ 1" pieces	150 g	5 oz	5 oz
Oil to fry			

Heat the oil in a deep frying pan on medium heat and fry the
cauliflower and potato pieces until they are golden brown. Place them
on a cooling tray and set them to one side.

Ingredients:	Metric	Imperial	American
Oil or ghee	75 ml	5 tbsp	5 tbsp
Mustard seeds	5 ml	1 tsp	1 tsp
Cumin seeds	5 ml	1 tsp	1 tsp
Large garlic cloves, crushed	5	5	5
Fresh ginger, finely chopped	4 cm	1½"	1½"
Medium onion, finely chopped	2	2	2
*Peppercorns	6	6	6
*Cloves	4	4	4
*Cinnamon stick	2.5 cm	1"	1"
Bay leaves	2	2	2
*Black cardamom	1	1	1
Ground coriander	10 ml	2 tsp	2 tsp
Garam masala	5 ml	1 tsp	1 tsp
Ground turmeric	2.5 ml	½ tsp	½ tsp

(handwritten: ½ tsp next to Fresh ginger; ½ tsp next to *Peppercorns)

Aloo, Gobhi and Gosht
(North Indian Style Potato, Cauliflower and Meat Curry)

DAY 10

Ground red chilli	2.5 ml	½ tsp	½ tsp
Salt to taste			
Canned tomatoes	400 g	14 oz	2 cups
To Garnish			
Garam masala	2.5 ml	½ tsp	½ tsp
Green coriander leaves, chopped	15 ml	1 tbsp	1 tbsp
Small green chilli, chopped	1	1	1

Cooking time: 35 minutes

- NOT FRYING

1 Heat the oil in a large heavy-bottomed saucepan on medium heat. Add the mustard seeds and when they start crackling brown the cumin seeds.
2 Put in the onion, garlic, ginger, bay leaves, cloves, peppercorns, cinnamon and black cardamom and gently fry until golden brown.
3 Add the meat pieces and fry for 5 minutes.
4 Stir in the coriander, garam masala, red chilli, turmeric, tomatoes and salt, and cook until all the liquid has been absorbed.
5 Pour in 50 ml/ 2 fl oz /3 ½ tbsp water and cook until all the water is absorbed. Put in 100 ml/ 3.5 fl oz water/ ½ cup water. Reduce the heat to low, close the lid simmer until the meat is tender.
6 Mix in the fried vegetables and cook on a low heat for a further 5 minutes.
7 Sprinkle over the garnish before serving.

Serving suggestion:
Serve hot with chapati, rice, rayta and dal.

Mixed Vegetable Korma
(South Indian Style)

Serves: 4-6

This delightfully refreshing dish has a distinct flavour of
coconut, fenugreek seeds, tamarind, spices and vegetables. This
is a medium hot recipe though South Indians generally make
their dishes very hot.

Ingredients:	Metric	Imperial	American
Small cauliflower, split into 2.5 cm/ 1" florets and washed	1	1	1
Small carrots, peeled, washed and cut into 4 cm/1 1/2 " pieces	6	6	6
Medium aubergine, washed, quartered and cut into 1.2 cm/ 1/2 " pieces	1	1	1
Medium green pepper, washed, quartered and cut into 1.2 cm/ 1/2 " pieces Peas	1	1	1 2/3 C.
Medium potato, peeled, washed and cut into 1 cm/ 1/2 " pieces	1	1	2
Oil	75 ml	5 tbsp	5 tbsp
Fenugreek seeds	5 ml	1 tsp	1 tsp
Mustard seeds	5 ml	1 tsp	1 tsp
Large garlic cloves	3	3	3
Fresh ginger, finely chopped	2.5 cm	1"	1"
Medium onion, finely chopped	1	1	1
Coconut desiccated, ground in a grinder	90 ml	6 tbsp	6 tbsp
Garam masala	5 ml	1 tsp	1 tsp
Ground coriander	5 ml	1 tsp	1 tsp
Ground roasted cumin	5 ml	1 tsp	1 tsp
Ground red chilli	2.5 ml	1/2 tsp	1/2 tsp
Ground turmeric	2.5 ml	1/2 tsp	1/2 tsp
Salt to taste			

Mixed Vegetable Korma
(South Indian Style)

DAY 10

Ingredients:

Ingredients:	Metric	Imperial	American
Canned tomatoes	*400 g*	*14 oz*	*2 cups*
Tamarind, extract pulp			
(See the recipe)	*50 g*	*2 oz*	*¹/₄ cup*
Water	*400 ml*	*14 fl oz*	*2 cups*
To Garnish			
Garam masala	*2.5 ml*	*¹/₂ tsp*	*¹/₂ tsp*
Green coriander leaves, chopped	*15 ml*	*1 tbsp*	*1 tbsp*
Small green chilli, chopped	*1*	*1*	*1*

Cooking time: 1 hour

1 Heat the oil in a large heavy-bottomed saucepan and brown the fenugreek and mustard seeds. Add the onion, garlic and the ginger and fry until golden brown.

2 Mix in the garam masala, coriander, roasted cumin, red chilli, turmeric and salt then the tomatoes and cook until all the liquid has been absorbed and the oil appears on the surface of the mixture.

3 Put in the cauliflower, carrot and 200 ml/7 fl oz/ 1 cup water. Bring to the boil. Reduce the heat to medium-low and cook for 15 minutes. Add the potato, aubergine, green pepper, rest of the water and the tamarind pulp and cook for a further 30 minutes or until the vegetables are tender.

4 Sprinkle over the garnish before serving.

Serving suggestion:

Serve hot with idli or puri, yoghurt, rice and dal.

Urud Ki Sukhi Dal
(White split urud lentil)

Serves: 4-6

Urud dal is not easy to digest therefore we must add asafoetida, ginger and garlic.
This dish is of medium hotness.

Ingredients:	Metric	Imperial	American
Urud dal, *cleaned and washed*	350 g	12 oz	12 oz
Ground turmeric	2.5 ml	$^1/_2$ tsp	$^1/_2$ tsp
Water	750 ml	1 $^1/_4$ cups	3 cups
Salt to taste			

Tarka

Ghee or oil	60 ml	4 tbsp	4 tbsp
Asafoetida	large pinch	$^1/_8$ tsp	$^1/_8$ tsp
Large garlic cloves, *crushed*	3	3	3
Fresh ginger, *chopped*	2.5 cm	1"	1"
Large onion, *finely chopped*	1	1	1
Ground roasted cumin	5 ml	1 tsp	1 tsp
Ground red chilli	2.5 ml	$^1/_2$ tsp	$^1/_2$ tsp
Ground turmeric	1.5 ml	$^1/_4$ tsp	$^1/_4$ tsp
Garam masala	2.5 ml	$^1/_2$ tsp	$^1/_2$ tsp

To garnish

Green coriander leaves, *chopped*	15 ml	1 tbsp	1 tbsp
Garam masala	2.5 ml	$^1/_2$ tsp	$^1/_2$ tsp
Small green chilli	1	1	1
Lemon cut into small pieces	1	1	1

Cooking time: 50 minutes

1 Place the washed lentil, turmeric, salt and the water into a large saucepan. Bring to the boil, skim off any scum and simmer on a low heat for 45 minutes or until the dal is tender.

Urud Ki Sukhi Dal
(White split urud lentil)

DAY 10

2 If any water is left, dry it off on a high heat but don't stir otherwise the dal will become mushy.

3 While the dal is cooking prepare the tarka. Heat the ghee in a heavy-bottomed saucepan. Add the asafoetida, garlic, ginger and the onion and fry gently on a medium heat until they are golden brown.

4 Add the garam masala, red chilli, turmeric and roasted cumin, and remove the pan from the heat and set it to one side.

5 Stir in the cooked dal.

6 Sprinkle over the garnish before serving.

Serving suggestion:

Serve hot with chapati or onion paratha, kerela (bitter gourd), stuffed aubergine, gajar-matar ki sabji (carrot and peas curry), potato curry and rayta.

DAY
11

In India we make paneer (Indian style cheese) at home. When it is cooked it becomes even more soft and spongy. This dish is often served during weddings or parties. Chicken Muglai is another royal dish which is liked by all my cookery class pupils. Tirangi barfi is a sweet which can be consumed after a meal or at tea time as a snack. It looks beautiful and tastes delicious.

Matar Paneer
(Peas and Indian Cheese)

Serves: 4-6

This dish is thoroughly enjoyed by both non-vegetarians and vegetarians. The paneer is very rich in protein. You will find this dish to be of medium hotness.

Ingredients:	Metric	Imperial	American
Paneer (see the recipe), use gold top milk	2.3 l	4 pt	10 cups
Peas, frozen or fresh (shelled)	500 g	1 lb 2 oz	4 cups
Ghee or oil	60 ml	4 tbsp	4 tbsp
Cumin seeds	5 ml	1 tsp	1 tsp
Small onion, finely chopped	1	1	1
Whole spices:			
*Cloves	4	4	4
*Peppercorns	4	4	4
Bay leaves	2	2	2
*Black cardamom	1	1	1
*Cinnamon	2.5 cm	1"	1"
Large garlic cloves	3	3	3
Fresh ginger	2.5 cm	1"	1"
Medium onion, cut into large pieces	1	1	1

Combine the last three ingredients in a blender and blend with 45 ml/ 3 tbsp water to make a smooth paste.

Ingredients:	Metric	Imperial	American
Ground coriander	10 ml	2 tsp	2 tsp
Garam masala	5 ml	1 tsp	1 tsp
Ground red chilli	2.5 ml	½ tsp	½ tsp
Ground turmeric	2.5 ml	½ tsp	½ tsp
Canned tomatoes	400 g	14 oz	2 cups
Salt to taste			

Tirangi Barfi
(Three coloured barfi)

DAY 11

Makes: 22

India got it's independence on 15th August 1947 and this auspicious day is celebrated throughout India. The Indian Tirangi (yellow, white and green) flag is waved everywhere. Tirangi barfies are distributed in schools and the shelves in sweet-shops are decorated with them. People buy, make and eat them with great pride.

Preparing the first layer (bottom):

Ingredients:	Metric	Imperial	American
Ghee, melted	10 ml	2 tsp	2 tsp
Full cream milk powder	50 g	2 oz	1/2 cup
Double fresh cream, whipped	60 ml	4 tbsp	4 tbsp

Place the cream and milk powder in a bowl with 5 ml/1 tsp of the ghee and mix thoroughly. Set the bowl on one side.

Pistachios, coarsely ground in a coffee grinder	25 g	1 oz	2 tbsp
Sugar	25 g	1 oz	2 tbsp
Water	25 ml	1 fl oz	1 fl oz
Food colour, green	2.5 ml	1/2 tsp	1/2 tsp
Essence, kevera or gulab water	2.5 ml	1/2 tsp	1/2 tsp
Large plate, greased with ghee	1	1	1

Total cooking time: 25 minutes

1 Place the pistachios and 5 ml/ 1 tsp of the ghee in a saucepan on a medium-low heat and fry for 3 minutes or until light brown. Add this to the milk powder mixture.

2 Place the sugar, water and food colour in the same saucepan on medium heat.

3 Boil it until it is ready to set (test by dropping a drop of syrup into a cup of cold water, if the drop sets and stays at the bottom it is ready).

Tirangi Barfi
(Three coloured barfi)

4 Stir in the milk powder mixture and the essence. Mix thoroughly until it is smooth and a little cool. Spread on the greased plate and shape into a square about 1.2 cm/ ½" thick.

Preparing the second layer (middle):

Ingredients:	Metric	Imperial	American
Ghee, melted	*10 ml*	*2 tsp*	*2 tsp*
Full cream milk powder	*50 g*	*2 oz*	*½ cup*
Double fresh cream, whipped	*60 ml*	*4 tbsp*	*4 tbsp*

Place the cream and milk powder in a bowl with 5 ml/1 tsp of the ghee and mix thoroughly. Set the bowl on one side.

Ingredients:	Metric	Imperial	American
Almonds, blanched, pat dry			
and coarsely ground in a			
coffee grinder	*25 g*	*1 oz*	*2 tbsp*
Sugar	*25 g*	*1 oz*	*2 tbsp*
Water	*25 ml*	*1 fl oz*	*1 fl oz*

1 Place the almonds and 5 ml/ 1 tsp of the ghee in a saucepan on a medium-low heat and fry for 3 minutes or until light brown. Add this to the milk powder mixture.
2 Place the sugar, and the water in the same saucepan on medium heat.
3 Boil it until it is ready to set (see first layer).
4 Stir in the milk powder mixture. Mix thoroughly until it is smooth and a little cool. Spread it over the first layer about 1.2 cm/ ½ " thick.

Tirangi Barfi
(Three coloured barfi)

DAY 11

Preparing the third layer (top)

Ingredients:	Metric	Imperial	American
Ghee, melted	10 ml	2 tsp	2 tsp
Full cream milk powder	50 g	2 oz	1/2 cup
Double fresh cream, whipped	60 ml	4 tbsp	4 tbsp
Ground green cardamom	2.5 ml	1/2 tsp	1/2 tsp

Place the cream, milk powder and cardamon in a bowl with 5 ml/ 1 tsp of the ghee and mix thoroughly. Set the bowl on one side.

Ingredients:	Metric	Imperial	American
Sweet coconut, desiccated	25 g	1 oz	2 tbsp
Sugar	25 g	1 oz	2 tbsp
Water	25 ml	1 fl oz	1 fl oz
Ground green cardamom	2.5 ml	1/2 tsp	1/2 tsp
Food colour, yellow	2.5 ml	1/2 tsp	1/2 tsp
Saffron	1.5 ml	1/4 tsp	1/4 tsp
Varak (fine, edible silver sheet)	1	1	1

1 Place the coconut and 5 ml/ 1 tsp of the ghee in a saucepan on a medium-low heat and fry for 3 minutes or until light brown. Add this to the milk powder mixture.
2 Place the sugar, water, colour, ground green cardamom and the saffron in the same saucepan on medium heat.
3 Boil it until it is ready to set (see first layer).
4 Stir in the milk powder mixture. Mix thoroughly until it is smooth and a little cool. Spread it over the second layer about 1.2 cm/ 1/2 " thick.
5 Cover with varak and leave to set in a cool place for 3-4 hours.
6 Cut into squares or triangles.

Serving suggestion:
Serve cold after a meal or at tea.

Over the last few years the Sweet and Sour Prawns dish has become increasingly popular in India. For this reason I felt I should introduce it in this book. The sauce can be used as a dip. Stuffed Aloo Paratha with pickle is also used for packed lunches and breakfast. It is quite amusing to see (if you get a chance to go to India) how many people will without fail eat an Aloo Paratha when travelling anywhere by train.

Dhandai is a cold milk drink with nuts. This is considered to be very healthy and whoever can afford the drink has it in both the hot and colder months.

Sweet and Sour Prawns

Serves: 4-5

This is another popular dish with my parents and brothers. The subtle blend of spices, honey and vinegar makes this an easy adaptable recipe to suit other meats i.e. pork or chicken. You will find this dish to be of medium hotness. (Sweet and sour chicken can be prepared simply by substituting the prawns for small pre-cooked chicken pieces.)

Ingredients:	Metric	Imperial	American
Prawns, shelled and washed	250 g	9 oz	9 oz
Vegetables: cauliflower, carrots, green pepper, aubergine or any other, washed and cut into 4 cm/ 1.5" pieces.	250 g	9 oz	9 oz

Batter:

Ingredients:	Metric	Imperial	American
Gram flour, sifted	100 g	4 oz	1 1/4 cups
Oil	15 ml	1 tbsp	1 tbsp
Green coriander leaves, chopped	15 ml	1 tbsp	1 tbsp
Tymol seeds	5 ml	1 tsp	1 tsp
Garam masala	5 ml	1 tsp	1 tsp
Ground red chilli	2.5 ml	1/2 tsp	1/2 tsp
Green chilli, chopped	1	1	1
Salt to taste			
Water, warm	150 ml	5 fl oz	2/3 cup

1 Place the sifted flour in a bowl and mix in the oil.
2 Add coriander leaves, green and red chilli; garam masala; salt; and tymol seeds.
3 Pour in the water to make a smooth batter.
Oil to Fry

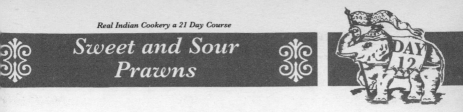

Sweet and Sour Prawns

DAY 12

Frying Time: 30 minutes

1 Heat the oil in a deep frying pan on medium heat.
2 Dip each cooked prawn piece in the batter and place gently in the hot oil.
3 Fry all the prawn pieces together until golden brown.
4 Remove the prawns with a slotted spoon and put them in a serving dish.
5 Now dip the vegetable pieces in the batter and fry 7-8 pieces together until golden brown.
6 Place them with the prawn pieces in the serving dish and set on one side.

Sauce:

Ingredients:	Metric	Imperial	American
Oil or Ghee	*75 ml*	*5 tbsp*	*5 tbsp*
Small onion, finely chopped	*1*	*1*	*1*
Large garlic cloves	*4*	*4*	*4*
Fresh ginger, coarsely chopped	*2.5 cm*	*1"*	*1"*
Medium onion, coarsely chopped	*1*	*1*	*1*

Combine the last three ingredients in a blender and blend to make a smooth paste.

Ingredients:	Metric	Imperial	American
Ground coriander	*10 ml*	*2 tsp*	*2 tsp*
Garam masala	*5 ml*	*1 tsp*	*1 tsp*
Ground roasted cumin	*5 ml*	*1 tsp*	*1 tsp*
Ground red chilli	*2.5 ml*	*1/2 tsp*	*1/2 tsp*
Ground tumeric	*2.5 ml*	*1/2 tsp*	*1/2 tsp*
Ground mace	*1.5 ml*	*1/4 tsp*	*1/4 tsp*
Ground nutmeg	*1.5 ml*	*1/4 tsp*	*1/4 tsp*
Salt to taste			
Canned tomatoes	*230 g*	*8 oz*	*2 cups*
Vinegar	*60 ml*	*4 tbsp*	*4 tbsp*

Sweet and Sour Prawns

Ingredients:	Metric	Imperial	American
Honey	*15 ml*	*1 tbsp*	*1 tbsp*
Water	*200 ml*	*7 fl oz*	*Scant 1 cup*

To Garnish

Garam masala	*2.5 ml*	*¹/₂ tsp*	*¹/₂ tsp*
Green coriander leaves, chopped	*15 ml*	*1 tbsp*	*1 tbsp*
Small green chilli, chopped	*1*	*1*	*1*

Cooking Time: 30 minutes

1 Heat the ghee in a heavy-bottomed saucepan and fry gently the chopped onions until golden brown.
2 Add the blended paste and fry until golden brown.
3 Put in garam masala, coriander, red chilli, tumeric, salt, nutmeg, mace, roasted cumin and the tomatoes.
4 Cook until all the liquid has been absorbed and the ghee appears on the surface of the mixture.
5 Pour in the vinegar and cook until all the liquid is absorbed.
6 Add the honey and cook for a further 2 minutes.
7 Finally add the water and bring to the boil.
8 Reduce the heat to low and simmer for 2 minutes.
9 Pour the hot sauce over the fried prawn and vegetable pieces just before you want to serve and sprinkle over the garnish. Dip your fried pieces in sauce while eating.

Serving Suggestions:

Serve hot with rice, puri, rayta and chutney.

Aloo Paratha
(Potato Paratha)

Makes: 11

This dish is often served at breakfast, and is delicious with natural yoghurt and pickle. This is also one of the breads which children take to school in their packed lunch boxes. You will find this recipe to be of medium hotness.

Preparing the dough:

Ingredients:	Metric	Imperial	American
Chapati flour, brown	275 g	10 oz	3 cups
Oil	15 ml	1 tbsp	1 tbsp
Salt	1.5 ml	¼ tsp	¼ tsp
Water, luke warm	150 ml	5 fl oz	⅔ cup

1 Place 250 g/9 oz flour into a bowl (keep the rest of the flour for rolling out). Rub the oil in it and add the salt.
2 Pour in the water to make a soft dough.
3 Knead it for 5 minutes or until the dough is soft, springy and satiny.
4 Cover and leave for 10 minutes.

Preparing the filling:

Ingredients:	Metric	Imperial	American
Potatoes boiled in jackets, peeled and mashed	500 g	1 lb 2 oz	18 oz
Green coriander leaves, chopped	30 ml	2 tbsp	2 tbsp
Lemon juice	15 ml	1 tbsp	1 tbsp
Garam masala	5 ml	1 tsp	1 tsp
Ground red chilli	2.5 ml	½ tsp	½ tsp
Tymol seeds, ajwain	2.5 ml	½ tsp	½ tsp
Fresh ginger, finely chopped	1 cm	½ "	½ "
Medium onion, finely chopped	1	1	1
Small green chilli, finely chopped	1	1	1
Salt to taste			

Aloo Paratha
(Potato Paratha)

DAY
12

Place all the above ingredients into a bowl and mix thoroughly. Divide into 11 equal portions.

Making the Paratha:

Oil to fry

Cooking Time: 35 minutes

1 Heat a flat frying pan on medium heat.
2 While the frying pan is heating divide the dough into 11 equal portions.
3 Take a portion of dough and roll it into a ball on the palm of your hands.
4 Dust it with flour, flatten it and roll it into a small round shape.
5 Place one portion of filling on it and cover bringing the edges together.
6 Again flatten, dust with flour and roll it into a round shape about 0.2 cm/ ⅛ " thick.
7 Place the aloo paratha on the hot frying pan and cook both sides dry like a chapati.
8 Then pour 7.5 ml/ ½ tbsp oil over it and fry the first side until light golden brown. Make 6 or 7 slits in the paratha.
9 Pour another 7.5 ml/ ½ tbsp oil and fry the other side light golden brown as well.

Serving Suggestions:

Serve hot with yoghurt, pickle and butter at breakfast. Take it for a picnic with stuffed aubergine, cauliflower or the pea-carrot dish and pickle.

DAY 12

Dhandai

Makes: 6 large glasses

Holi is the Hindu's most exciting festival. It takes place in April to celebrate the victory of God and destruction of demons. People visit each others homes to play with gulal (dry coloured powder with a sparkling substance in it) and to throw coloured water at each other. They sing and dance on their way between houses. The host graciously offers them lots of sweets and snacks to eat and 'Dhandai' to drink.

Ingredients:	Metric	Imperial	American
Milk	1.1 l	2 pt	5 cups
Sugar	50 g	2 oz	¼ cup
Almonds, blanched	25 g	1 oz	2 tbsp
Pistachios	15 g	½ oz	1 tbsp

Combine the almonds and pistachios in a coffee grinder and grind to a fine powder.

Ingredients:	Metric	Imperial	American
Essence, kevera or gulab water	5 ml	1 tsp	1 tsp
Optional food colour, yellow	2.5 ml	½ tsp	½ tsp
Ground green cardamom	1.5 ml	¼ tsp	¼ tsp
Saffron	1.5 ml	¼ tsp	¼ tsp
Ground mace	1.5 ml	¼ tsp	¼ tsp
Ground nutmeg	1.5 ml	¼ tsp	¼ tsp
Ice to Chill			

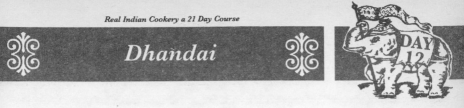

Dhandai

1 Pour the milk in a large jug. Add the sugar and mix until
   dissolved.
2 Stir in the rest of the ingredients, essence and the ice.

Serving Suggestions:
Serve cold instead of tea during the summer or with a meal.

DAY
13

Today you will meet some of the most
attractive and delicious dishes of a
vegetarian banquet.

The whole cauliflower surrounded by
potato is enough to make anyone's
mouth water.

Carrot Halwa is a very nourishing
sweet dish - it is
so popular that there is even
a book entitled "Dadi ji's Carrot
Halwa" (Grandmother's Carrot
Halwa). It originates from the North of
India - North Indians love rich food.
Chicken Curry is another dish which
is constantly admired by those
I have catered for.

DAY 13

Chicken Curry

Serves: 4-6

This recipe is of medium hotness and is very tasty and flavourful. One can taste a lot of Indian herbs. If one wants to eat this with rice the gravy must be fairly liquid, however with chapati this should be quite thick.

Ingredients:	Metric	Imperial	American
Chicken, thigh and drum sticks			
cut into 12 pieces	1 kg	2 lb 3 oz	2 lb 3 oz
Oil or ghee	75 ml	5 tbsp	5 tbsp
Medium onion, thinly sliced	2	2	2
Large garlic, chopped	5	5	5
*Cinnamon stick	1.2 cm	½ "	½ "
*Cloves	4	4	4
*Peppercorns	4	4	4
*Black cardamom	1	1	1
Bay leaves	2	2	2
Aniseed	15 ml	1 tbsp	1 tbsp
Ground almond	15 ml	1 tbsp	1 tbsp
Ground coriander	15 ml	1 tbsp	1 tbsp
Garam masala	5 ml	1 tsp	1 tsp
Ground cumin, roasted	5 ml	1 tsp	1 tsp
Ground red chilli	2.5 ml	½ tsp	½ tsp
Ground turmeric	2.5 ml	½ tsp	½ tsp
Tomatoes, tinned	400 g	14 oz	14 oz
Salt to taste			
Yoghurt	150 g	5 oz	1 cup

Chicken Curry

To Garnish:

Ingredients:	Metric	Imperial	American
Garam masala	2.5 ml	¹/₂ tsp	¹/₂ tsp
Green coriander leaves, chopped	15 ml	1 tbsp	1 tbsp
Small green chilli, chopped	1	1	1

Cooking Time: 55

1 Heat the oil in a heavy-bottomed large saucepan.
2 Add the onion, garlic, bay leaves, ginger, and the whole spices and fry gently until the onion is golden brown on a medium heat.
3 Then add the chicken pieces and fry until they are lightly golden brown on all sides.
4 Stir in the aniseed, ground almonds, coriander, garam masala, roasted cumin, red chilli, turmeric, tomatoes, salt and cook until all the water has been absorbed and the oil appears on the surface of the mixture.
5 Then add the yoghurt and cook until all the liquid is absorbed.
6 Put 100 ml/ 3 ¹/₂ fl oz water. Cover the pan and simmer on a low heat for about 20 minutes, stirring a few times until the chicken is tender.
7 Finally add 75 ml/ 3 fl oz water. Increase the heat to medium and cook the chicken curry for a further 2 minutes or until required thickness of gravy is obtained. Sprinkle over the garnish before serving

Serving Suggestion:

Serve hot with chapati or rice, cauliflower, beans and potato sabji, dahibara and chutney.

Sabat Gobhi
(Whole Cauliflower)

Serves: 4-6

Sabat gobhi is a vegetarian party dish (and is equivalent to the whole roasted or tandoori chicken dish). For best results one needs a fresh and firm cauliflower.

This dish is of medium hotness.

Ingredients:	Metric	Imperial	American
Medium firm cauliflower, cut all the leaves and the stalk of the cauliflower and wash	1	1	1
Oil to fry			
Ghee or oil	60 ml	4 tbsp	4 tbsp
Mustard seeds	5 ml	1 tsp	1 tsp
Medium onion, finely chopped	1	1	1
*Cloves	4	4	4
*Peppercorns	4	4	4
Bay leaves	3	3	3
*Cinnamon stick	2.5 ml	1"	1"
*Black cardamom	1	1	1
Large garlic cloves	3	3	3
Fresh ginger, chopped	4 cm	1 1/2 "	1 1/2 "
Medium onion, chopped	1	1	1

Combine the the last three ingredients in a blender with 45 ml/ 3 tbsp water and blend to make a smooth paste.

Ingredients:	Metric	Imperial	American
Ground coriander	10 ml	2 tsp	2 tsp
Ground roasted cumin	5 ml	1 tsp	1 tsp
Garam masala	5 ml	1 tsp	1 tsp
Ground turmeric	5 ml	1 tsp	1 tsp
Ground red chilli	2.5 ml	1/2 tsp	1/2 tsp
Ground mace	1.5 ml	1/4 tsp	1/4 tsp

Sabat Gobhi
(Whole Cauliflower)

DAY 13

Ground nutmeg	1.5 ml	¹/₄ tsp	¹/₄ tsp
Salt to taste			
Tomatoes, tinned	400 g	14 oz	14 oz

To Garnish:

Ingredients:	Metric	Imperial	American
Potatoes, peeled, washed and cut lengthwise for chips	350 g	12 oz	12 oz
Peas frozen (or fresh, shelled)	225 g	8 oz	2 cups
Green coriander leaves, chopped	30 ml	2 tbsp	2 tbsp
Garam masala	5 ml	1 tsp	1 tsp
Small green chilli, chopped	1	1	1

Cooking Time: 55 minutes

1 Heat the oil in a deep frying pan and fry the whole cauliflower on a medium heat until golden brown on all sides. Take it out and keep the cauliflower on one side.

2 Heat the ghee in a large heavy-bottomed frying pan and add the mustard seeds. When they start crackling, add the chopped onion, bay leaves and the whole spices and fry until golden brown on a medium heat.

3 Mix in the blended paste and fry for a further few minutes until golden brown.

4 Stir in garam masala, coriander, turmeric, mace, nutmeg, roasted cumin, red chilli and salt and then the tomatoes and fry until all the liquid has been absorbed and the ghee appears on the surface of the mixture.

5 Put in the 50 ml/ 2 fl oz water and cook until all the water is absorbed.

6 Place the fried cauliflower in the frying pan and gently base with the sauce and cook on a low heat. Turn the cauliflower over gently after 5 minutes, cooking and basting with the sauce until the cauliflower is cooked.

Sabat Gobhi
(Whole Cauliflower)

7 While the cauliflower is cooking fry the chips in a deep frying pan until golden brown. Boil the peas until tender.

Garnish Suggestion:

Place the cooked cauliflower with sauce in a large serving dish and spread around the chips and the peas. Sprinkle over the garam masala, coriander leaves and the chilli before serving.

Serving Suggestion:

Serve hot with puri, dal, pulao and dahibara.

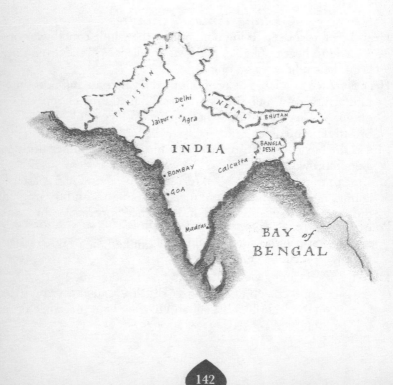

Gajar Ka Halwa
(North Indian-Punjabi style)
(Carrot Halwa)

Serves: 8

Gajar ka halwa is one of the most attractive, delicious and nourishing sweet dishes from North India

Ingredients:	Metric	Imperial	American
Carrots, scraped, washed and grated	*900 g*	*2 lb*	*2 lb*
Milk	*575 ml*	*1 pt*	*2 ¹/₂ cups*
Ghee	*60 ml*	*4 tbsp*	*4 tbsp*
Sugar	*200 g*	*7 oz*	*1 cup*
Khoya (see the recipe)	*150 g*	*5 oz*	*5 oz*
Almonds, blanched and cut into halves lengthwise	*50 g*	*2 oz*	*¹/₃ cup*
Sultanas	*50 g*	*2 oz*	*¹/₃ cup*
Pistachios, cut into halves lengthwise	*25 g*	*1 oz*	*2 tbsp*
Ground green cardamom	*5 ml*	*1 tsp*	*1 tsp*

Cooking time: 50 minutes

1 Place the carrot and the milk in a large heavy-bottomed saucepan on a high heat. Bring to the boil.

2 Reduce the heat to medium, stirring occasionally and cook until all the milk has been absorbed.

3 Add the sugar (it will make the carrot watery), green cardamom and cook again until all the liquid is absorbed.

4 Pour in the ghee. Reduce the heat to medium-low and fry for 10 minutes. Stir in the chopped nuts, sultanas and the khoya and cook for a further 5 minutes.

Serving Suggestion:
Serve hot after a meal.

Today again I'll take you to the South of India. Sambar is a nourishing mouthwatering lentil dish prepared with vegetables. In South India people usually use whole green chilli and make it quite hot but I suggest you make it according to your own taste so that the flavour of the spices can be relished. One can enjoy Sambar with plain rice, but you can add extra flavour to your meal if you prepare idli. Coconut chutney is another must with the above dishes. I normally put plenty of lentils on idli or rice.

Rogan Josh is prepared in Kashmiri Style. This dish is highly popular with my cookery class. Rogan Mirch is a type of chilli which adds more colour to a dish than hotness.

Serves: 4-6

This delicious dish is very popular among the Kashmiri community and among the members of my classes. You will find this dish to be of medium hotness.

Ingredients:	Metric	Imperial	American
Lamb, boned, cut into 4 cm/ 1 ½" pieces fat trimmed and washed	500 g	1 lb 2 oz	18 oz
Ghee or oil	75 ml	5 tbsp	5 tbsp
Onion seeds	5 ml	1 tsp	1 tsp
Large garlic cloves, crushed	4	4	4
Bay leaves	3	3	3
Fresh ginger, finely chopped	2.5 cm	1"	1"
Medium onion, finely chopped	1	1	1
Whole coriander	15 ml	1 tbsp	1 tbsp
Cumin seeds	5 ml	1 tsp	1 tsp
Poppy seeds	5 ml	1 tsp	1 tsp
Cloves	4	4	4
Peppercorns	4	4	4
Cinnamon stick	2.5 cm	1"	1"
Black cardamom, use seeds only	2	2	2

Heat a flat frying pan on medium heat and roast the last seven spices until golden brown. Leave to cool and then grind in a coffee grinder to a powder.

Ingredients:	Metric	Imperial	American
Coconut desiccated (or fresh, grated)	15 ml	1 tbsp	1 tbsp
Almond powder	15 ml	1 tbsp	1 tbsp
Ground mace	1.5 ml	¼ tsp	¼ tsp
Ground nutmeg	1.5 ml	¼ tsp	¼ tsp

Rogan Josh
(Kashmiri Style)

DAY 14

Heat a flat frying pan on medium heat and roast these ingredients until light brown.

Ground red chilli or *rogni mirch*	2.5 ml	¹/₂ tsp	¹/₂ tsp
Ground turmeric	2.5 ml	¹/₂ tsp	¹/₂ tsp
Salt to taste			
Tomatoes, canned	230 g	8 oz	1 cup
Yoghurt, natural	150 g	5 oz	²/₃ cup
Green pepper (cut in 1" pieces)	1	1	1
Water	200 ml	7 fl oz	7 fl oz
Lemon	30 ml	2 tbsp	2 tbsp
Sugar	15 ml	1 tbsp	1 tbsp
To Garnish:			
Garam masala	2.5 ml	¹/₂ tsp	¹/₂ tsp
Green coriander leaves, chopped	15 ml	1 tbsp	1 tbsp
Small green chilli, chopped	1	1	1

Cooking Time: 40 minutes

1 Heat the ghee in a large heavy-bottomed saucepan on medium heat. Add the onion seeds and fry them for 30 seconds. Put in the onion, garlic, ginger and the bay leaves and fry until golden brown.
2 Mix in the meat pieces and fry for 5 minutes.
3 Stir in the red chilli, turmeric, salt and the roasted ingredients and then the tomatoes and cook until all the liquid has been absorbed and the ghee appears on the surface of the mixture.
4 Add the yoghurt and cook again until all the liquid has diminished.
5 Pour in the water, bring to the boil, reduce the heat to low, close the lid and cook for 10 minutes.
6 Add lemon juice and sugar and further cook for 1 minute.
7 Sprinkle over the garnish before serving.

Serving Suggestion:
Serve hot with chapati, rayta, dal and rice.

Sambar
(South Indian Style)

Serves: 4-6

This popular South Indian dish is admired in all parts of India.
To make it as hot as the authentic South Indian dish add
double the quantity of red chilli.

Ingredients:	Metric	Imperial	American
Sambar Masala:			
Coconut desiccated (or fresh, grated)	50 g	2 oz	4 tbsp
Oil	10 ml	2 tsp	2 tsp
Whole coriander, cleaned	15 ml	1 tbsp	1 tbsp
Urud ki dhuli dal, cleaned	10 ml	2 tsp	2 tsp
Gram dal (split yellow peas), cleaned	10 ml	2 tsp	2 tsp
Fenugreek seeds	5 ml	1 tsp	1 tsp
Whole small dried red chilli	4	4	4

Heat the oil in a flat frying pan on a medium-low heat and roast all
the ingredients for 5 minutes or until light brown. Cool it and grind
to a fine powder.

Ingredients:	Metric	Imperial	American
Sambar:			
Arhar dal (tuvar dal), cleaned, washed and drained	250 g	9 oz	9 oz
Ground turmeric	5 ml	1 tsp	1 tsp
Salt to taste			
Water	1.1 l	2 pt	5 cups
Aubergine (or okra), washed, quartered and cut into 42 pieces	250 g	9 oz	9 oz
Tamarind, extract the pulp (see recipe page 26)	75 g	3 oz	3 oz
Tarka:			
Oil	90 ml	6 tbsp	6 tbsp

Sambar
(South Indian Style)

Ingredients:	Metric	Imperial	American
Asafoetida	*large pinch*	*large pinch*	*large pinch*
Mustard seeds	*5 ml*	*1 tsp*	*1 tsp*
Curry leaves or bay leaves	*3*	*3*	*3*
Small onion, thinly sliced	*3*	*3*	*3*
Garam masala	*5 ml*	*1 tsp*	*1 tsp*
Tomatoes, tinned	*400 g*	*14 oz*	*14 oz*
Green coriander leaves	*90 ml*	*6 tbsp*	*6 tbsp*

Cooking Time: 40 minutes

1 Place the dal, salt, turmeric and the water into a large saucepan. Bring to the boil, skim off any scum, reduce the heat to medium-low, close the lid and simmer for 30 minutes or until the dal is tender.
2 While the dal is cooking, cook the aubergine or okra in the tamarind pulp, bring to the boil and add the sambar masala.
3 Cook on a medium-low heat for 10 minutes or until the aubergine (or any other vegetable) is tender.
4 Mix in the cooked dal.
5 Heat the oil in a saucepan on a medium heat for the tarka (prepare the tarka as well while the dal is cooking). Add the asafoetida and the mustard seeds. When the mustard seeds start crackling put in the onion and the curry leaves and fry them until lightly brown.
6 Stir in the garam masala and the tomatoes and cook until all the liquid has been absorbed and the oil appears on the surface of the mixture.
7 Add the coriander leaves. Mix in the cooked dal. Bring to the boil, reduce the heat to low and simmer for 5 minutes.

Serving Suggestion:
Serve hot with dosa or idli or rice, rayta and stuffed bitter-gourd or cauliflower-potato.

149

Idli
(South Indian bread)

Makes: 12

This plain rice and lentil bread cooked in steam is the speciality of South India. It goes superbly with hot sambar and coconut chutney. A South Indian meal is not complete without idli.

Ingredients:	Metric	Imperial	American
Rice, cleaned, washed and soaked overnight	150 g	5 oz	1 cup
Urud ki dhuli dal, cleaned, washed and soaked	75 g	3 oz	½ cup
Water	225 ml	8 fl oz	1 cup

Combine the above ingredients in a blender and blend them to make a thick smooth paste.

Salt	large pinch	large pinch	large pinch

Add the salt to the lentil and rice paste and whip this for 5 minutes. Cover and keep in a warm place for 24 hrs.

Cooking time: 35 minutes

1 Boil some water (water level should be under idli containers) in a large saucepan.
2 Grease idli containers with a little oil.
3 Pour 30 ml/ 2 tbsp idli mixture into the containers.
4 Close the lid and steam cook for 30 minutes or until tender.

Serving Suggestions:

Serve hot with sambar, coconut chutney and vegetable korma.

DAY
15

Dhansank is another popular dish which is enjoyed by both vegetarians (without chicken pieces) and non vegetarians. After cooking one can either purée the lentils and vegetables or leave it as it is.

This method of preparing okra is quick and easy. Because it is a dry dish it is highly suitable for any type of packed lunch or picnic. Another advantage of its dry nature is that it does not go off quickly. Vermichelli is a sweet dish which is very simple and easy to make. Likewise Sabudana Papadoms are easy to make. These can be stored.

DAY 15

Dhansank

Serves: 4-6

This delightful dish is cooked with different varieties of
lentils and vegetables. Dhansank is not only delicious
but rich in food minerals.

Ingredients:	Metric	Imperial	American
Chicken (boned), skinned, cut into 5 cm/ 2" pieces and washed	800 g	1 ½ lb	1 ½ lb
Dals (use 5 or 6 types of different lentils - moong (split yellow peas), gram, masoor (red lentils), tuvar, green whole moong and black whole urud), weighing about 25 g/ 1 oz each cleaned, soaked overnight and washed	150 g	6 oz	6 oz
Ground turmeric	2.5 ml	½ tsp	½ tsp
Salt to taste			
Vegetables (use 4 different - e.g. green pepper, aubergine, mushroom and marrow, peeled, washed and cut into large pieces	200 g	7 oz	7 oz
Methi (green fenugreek leaves), use leaves only	45 ml	3 tbsp	3 tbsp
Mint leaves, use leaves only	45 ml	3 tbsp	3 tbsp
Coriander leaves, used leaves only	45 ml	3 tbsp	3 tbsp
Coconut desiccated or fresh, grated	30 ml	2 tbsp	2 tbsp
Large garlic cloves, crushed	5	5	5
Fresh ginger, finely chopped	2.5 cm	1"	1"
Medium onion, finely chopped	1	1	1
Water	900 ml	1 ½ pt	3 ⅔ cups

Dhansank

DAY 15

Ingredients:	Metric	Imperial	American
Ghee or oil	90 ml	6 tbsp	½ cup
Mustard seeds	5 ml	1 tsp	1 tsp
Cumin seeds	5 ml	1 tsp	1 tsp
Medium onion, finely chopped	1	1	1
Garam masala	10 ml	2 tsp	2 tsp
Ground coriander	10 ml	2 tsp	2 tsp
Ground roasted cumin	5 ml	1 tsp	1 tsp
Ground red chilli	5 ml	1 tsp	1 tsp
Ground sambar masala	15 ml	1 tbsp	1 tsp
(see miscellaneous recipe page 25)			
Ground turmeric	2.5 ml	½ tsp	½ tbsp
Salt to taste			
Tomatoes, canned	400 g	14 oz	14 oz
Lemon juice	60 ml	4 tbsp	4 tbsp
Water	150 ml	5 fl oz	⅔ cup

To Garnish:

Garam masala	2.5 ml	½ tsp	½ tsp
Small green chilli, chopped	1	1	1

Cooking Time: 1 hour 10 minutes

1 Place the chicken, dal, turmeric, salt, vegetables, methi, mint,
   coriander, coconut, onion, garlic and the ginger with 900 ml/
   1 ½ pints/ 3 ⅔ cups of water on a medium heat. Bring to the
   boil, skim off any scum, reduce the heat to medium-low, close
   the lid and cook for 40 minutes or until the chicken is tender.
2 Take out the chicken pieces and cook the lentil mixture for a
   further 20 minutes or until the lentils are tender.
3 Leave it to cool and then put in a blender to make a smooth paste.
4 While the lentil mixture is cooking heat the ghee in a saucepan on
   a medium heat. Add the mustard seeds and when they start
   crackling, brown the cumin seeds. Put in the onion and gently
   fry until golden brown.

DAY 15

Dhansank

5 Mix in the cooked chicken pieces and fry for 5 minutes or until light brown.
6 Stir in the garam masala, coriander, roasted cumin, red chilli, sambar masala, turmeric, salt, tomatoes and cook for a further 2 minutes.
7 Pour in the ground lentil paste, lemon juice and 150 ml/5 fl oz/ ⅔ cup water. Bring to the boil, reduce the heat to medium-low and cook for a further 10 minutes or until the required consistency is obtained.
Sprinkle over the garnish before serving.

Serving Suggestion:
Serve hot with rice, puri, vegetable kofta and rayta.

Fried Bhindi or Okra
(North Indian Style-Lady's finger)

DAY 15

Serves: 4

Cooked in this way bhindi is delicious and crispy, don't be put off by the sticky nature of the fresh vegetable.

Ingredients:	Metric	Imperial	American
Tender lady's finger, washed, dried, the ends trimmed and cut into 1 cm / ½ " round pieces	500 g	18 oz	18 oz
Oil	75 ml	5 tbsp	5 tbsp
Medium onion, finely chopped	3	3	3
Fresh ginger, finely chopped	2.5 cm	1"	1"
Ground coriander	15 ml	1 tbsp	1 tbsp
Ground roasted cumin	5 ml	1 tsp	1 tsp
Ground turmeric	2.5 ml	½ tsp	½ tsp
Ground red chilli	2.5 ml	½ tsp	½ tsp
Garam masala	2.5 ml	½ tsp	½ tsp
Salt to taste			

To Garnish:

Garam masala	2.5 ml	½ tsp	½ tsp
Small green chilli	1	1	1

Cooking Time: 20 minutes

1 Heat the oil in a frying pan on medium heat and lightly brown the onion and the ginger.
2 Add the okra pieces and fry for a further 5 minutes.
3 Add the coriander, cumin, turmeric, red chilli, garam masala and salt; cook on low heat for a further 5-7 minutes or until tender. Keep turning them over.
4 Sprinkle over the garnish before serving.

Serving Suggestion:

Serve hot with paratha or puri, dal, rayta, rice and a meat dish.

Sabudana Papar
(Tapioca papadum)

Makes: 22

Sabudana papadoms are quite easy to make and they compliment all sorts of meals. I have made them very mild but one can add coarsely ground peppercorns and ground red chilli (according to taste) to make them hot.

Ingredients:	Metric	Imperial	American
Tapioca	50 g	2 oz	2 oz
Salt	1.5 ml	1/4 tsp	1/4 tsp
Water	500 ml	18 fl oz	18 fl oz
Food colour, yellow, red, green or blue (optional)			
Large oblong or round tray, greased with oil	2	2	2
Oil to fry			

Cooking Time: 10 minutes

1 Place the tapioca, water and the salt (a food colour if you are making them coloured) in a saucepan on medium heat. Stir it continuously until all the water has been absorbed (one can check this in two ways - (i) While stirring, the mixture will leave the edge of the pan. (ii) If you drop a little cooked topioca from a spoon, it joins together and falls in a lump).

2 Turn the heat off. Take 15 ml/ 1 tbsp cooked topioca and place it on the tray (it will spread very thinly itself about 7.5 cm/ 3" in diameter circle. If it doesn't it means you have over cooked it. Don't worry, add an extra 100 ml/ 3 ½ fl oz/ 6 ½ tbsp water and boil it again).

3 Place 11 papars on one tray. Leave them to dry.

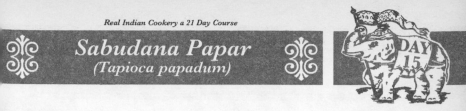

Sabudana Papar
(Tapioca papadum)

4 On the next day they will be loose on the tray. Turn them over. After drying, the tapioca papar shrinks in size.

5 Heat the oil in a deep frying pan on medium-high heat. When the oil is very hot gently slip a dried papar in the hot oil and it will increase 3 times in size. Fry it very light brown on both sides (it will take a few seconds only). Fry them before serving and they will be crispy and crunchy. Do not fry too far in advance because papars tend to go soft very quickly.

Serving Suggestions:
Serve hot or at room temperature with a meal or at tea time.

Preservation:
When completely dried keep them in an airtight container.

DAY
16

Today you will meet some items of the chāt family. Chāt is popular all over India. It is sold on the roadside, served in restaurants and even in smart hotels. Chāt can be eaten at any time by anyone - on plates and on leaves, with a fork or with the hand. As in this country, children spend their money on chocolate, in the same way in India, children spend their money on chāt. One can always see a long queue in front of the chat stalls. Chāt is spicy, crunchy, and sweet and sour in taste.

Aloo Ki Tikiya
(North Indian Style-Potato Patties)

Makes: 12

Tikiya is an appetizing item for tea and for chāt especially
during winter and the rainy seasons. They are very easy to
make and one can buy them from hawkers in the streets and
railway stations of India. You will find this dish to be of
medium hotness.

Preparing the potato coating:

Ingredients:	Metric	Imperial	American
Potatoes, boiled in jackets, peeled and mashed	500 g	1 lb 2 oz	5 cups
Green coriander leaves, chopped	15 ml	1 tbsp	1 tbsp
Garam masala	2.5 ml	1/2 tsp	1/2 tsp
Ground red chilli	2.5 ml	1/2 tsp	1/2 tsp
Ground roasted cumin	2.5 ml	1/2 tsp	1/2 tsp
Small green chilli, chopped (optional)	1	1	1
Salt to taste			

Place the above ingredients in a bowl. Mix them together thoroughly
and divide into 12 equal portions.

Preparing the peas filling:

Ingredients:	Metric	Imperial	American
Peas, fresh or frozen	250 g	9 oz	2 1/4 cups
Oil	30 ml	2 tbsp	2 tbsp
Mustard seeds	2.5 ml	1/2 tsp	1/2 tsp
Cumin seeds	5 ml	1 tsp	1 tsp
Garam masala	5 ml	1 tsp	1 tsp
Ground coriander	5 ml	1 tsp	1 tsp
Ground roasted cumin	5 ml	1 tsp	1 tsp
Ground red chilli	1.5 ml	1/4 tsp	1/4 tsp
Salt to taste			

Aloo Ki Tikiya
(North Indian Style-Potato Patties)

DAY 16

Ingredients:	Metric	Imperial	American
Lemon juice	*30 ml*	*2 tbsp*	*2 tbsp*
Green coriander leaves, chopped	*15 ml*	*1 tbsp*	*1 tbsp*
Green chilli, chopped	*1*	*1*	*1*

1 Heat the oil in a heavy-bottomed saucepan. Add the mustard seeds and when they start crackling, brown the cumin seeds.
2 Stir in the red chilli, ground cumin, ground coriander, salt and the peas.
3 When the peas are cooked add the lemon juice, garam masala, green chilli and the coriander leaves. Mix them and set the pan on one side. Divide into 12 equal portions.

Preparing the tikias:

Oil to fry

Frying Time: 35 minutes

1 Take one portion of the mashed potato and roll it into a ball in the palm of your hands, flatten the ball and place a portion of the peas filling into the centre. Bring the edges over and smoothly cover the filling. Make into a ball again and flatten until it is a 1 cm/ ½ " thick circle. Repeat and finish the mixture.
2 Heat a flat frying pan on a medium heat and smear with 30 ml/ 2 tablespoons of oil. Place 5 - 6 tikiyas on it.
3 When the underneath is golden brown, turn them over carefully.
4 Pour 15 - 30 ml/ 1 -2 tablespoons more all around the tikiiyas and fry the other side as well until golden brown.

Serving Suggestion:

1 Serve hot with chutney, gulabjamun, balushahi and dalmond at tea.
2 Serve it as a *"Chāt"*:- cut tikya in half, crush a papri or two golguppas and sprinkle over it, pour 15 ml/ 1 tbsp whisked natural yoghurt and 5 ml/ 1 tsp tamarind chutney over it. Sprinkle garam masala, red chilli, ground roasted cumin over and eat it.

Gol Guppa

Makes: 24

Gol guppa are one of the delicious items of the "*chāt*". It is difficult to find a single street in India where a hawker is not selling chat. In the main shopping areas, one finds several hawkers sitting next to each other (as close as 2 yards apart) selling this popular snack.

Preparing the filling:

Ingredients:	Metric	Imperial	American
Chickpeas, boiled (see the recipe)	75 g	3 oz	¹/₂ cup
Potatoes, boiled in jackets, peeled and cut into tiny pieces	75 g	3 oz	3 oz
Green coriander leaves, chopped	15 ml	1 tbsp	1 tbsp
Salt to taste			

Place the above ingredients into a bowl. Mix them thoroughly and set the bowl on one side (I normally boil extra chickpeas so that I can make Khatéwalé Kabuli Chunna as well see page 56).

Preparing the gol guppa:

Prepare the gol guppa while the chickpeas and potatoes are boiling.

Brown chapati flour (wheat flour)	50 g	2 oz	¹/₂ cup
Semolina	25 g	1 oz	¹/₄ cup
Lemon juice	2.5 ml	¹/₂ tsp	¹/₂ tsp
Salt	small pinch	small pinch	small pinch
Water, luke warm	50 ml	2 fl oz	¹/₄ cup

Place the above ingredients in a bowl. Mix thoroughly. Knead the dough with the warm water for 3 - 5 minutes or until the dough is springy and satiny. Cover and leave for 30 minutes.

1 Roll the dough into a ball with the palm of your hands. Flatten it, place a few drops of oil on the rolling board and then roll into a thin circle.

2 Cut several circles of 6 cm/ 2¹/₄ " in diameter. Repeat until you have used all the dough.

3 Take a teacloth and soak it in water.

Gol Guppa

4 Spread it on an up turned tray. Spread the small circles on the tea-cloth and cover with another wet teacloth and leave for 5 minutes.

Cooking Time: 30 minutes

1 Heat the oil in a deep frying pan on medium heat. Put one circle into the hot oil, sinking it gently under the oil using a slotted spoon. As soon as it comes up like a balloon, put another one in.
2 Fry four or five together until golden brown and crispy. Keep them turning over.
3 Leave them to cool on a cooling tray. The gol guppas can be kept for two weeks in an airtight tin.

Preparing the gol guppa ka pani (spicy water of the gol guppa):

Ingredients:	Metric	Imperial	American
Water (pani)	300 ml	1/2 pt	1 1/4 cups
Sugar	10 ml	2 tsp	2 tsp
Garam masala	2.5 ml	1/2 tsp	1/2 tsp
Ground red chilli	2.5 ml	1/2 tsp	1/2 tsp
Ground roasted cumin	2.5 ml	1/2 tsp	1/2 tsp
Tamarind pulp, thick	15 ml	1 tbsp	1 tbsp
Lemon juice	15 ml	1 tbsp	1 tbsp
Green coriander leaves	15 ml	1 tbsp	1 tbsp
Fresh mint	15 ml	1 tbsp	1 tbsp
Salt to taste			

1 Combine the coriander and mint leaves in a blender and blend with 60 ml/ 4 tbsp water until a smooth paste.
2 Pour the water into a jug and add all the above ingredients. Mix it thoroughly.
3 Dilute to your taste and keep in a refrigerator for 2-3 hours before using.

Serving Suggestion:

Make a small hole in each gol guppa and fill it with the filling mixture. Dip it in the pani or pour the pani in it and eat at once otherwise it will be soggy. We put whole gol guppas in our mouths!

Papri

Makes: 24

The papri can be eaten as a snack or as one of the items of chāt. It is very crispy and delicious. In India young girls spend most of their pocket money on chāt and then on a chocolate or a sweet. In every school and college, one will find at least one chāt stall with a long queue of keen buyers during lunch time and later in front of the chāt hawkers outside the school.

Ingredients:	Metric	Imperial	American
Plain flour, sifted	250 g	8 oz	2 ¼ cups
Lemon juice	5 ml	1 tsp	1 tsp
Tymol seeds (ajwain)	5 ml	1 tsp	1 tsp
Water, (luke warm)	125 ml	4 fl oz	½ cup
Salt	1.5 ml	¼ tsp	¼ tsp

Place 200g/ 7 oz /1 ¼ cups of the flour and the rest of the ingredients in a bowl. Knead the dough with water for 5 minutes or until the dough is soft, springy and satiny. Cover and leave it for 30 minutes.

Oil to fry

Cooking Time: 40 minutes

1 Divide the dough into 24 equal portions. Take a portion and roll it into a ball in the palm of your hands, flatten it, put a few drops of oil on the rolling board and roll it into a thin circle.
2 Smear the top with 2.5 ml/ ½ tsp of oil, sprinkle with dry flour and fold in half (giving a half moon shape).
3 Smear the top again with oil and sprinkle on the dry flour and fold again. Then roll the whole thing out thinly in a triangle shape about ½ cm/ ¼ " thick.
4 Heat the oil in a deep frying pan on a medium-low heat. Slip 4-5 paparies gently into the hot oil from the edge of the pan.

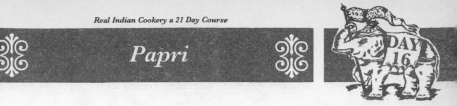

Papri

DAY 16

5 Keep turning them over and fry until light brown and crispy. Roll the paparies for the next batch while one batch is frying.

Serving Suggestion:

Serve it as it is at tea or serve it as a "Chāt". Place one tablespoon of gol guppaís filling (see the recipe) on the papari. Pour 15 ml/ 1 tbsp whisked natural yoghurt and 5 ml/ 1 tsp tamarind chutney over it. Sprinkle garam masala, red chilli, ground roasted cumin over and eat at once otherwise it will become soggy.

Preserving suggestions:

Will keep for a fortnight in an air tight tin or container.

Fruit Chāt

Serves: 4-6

Fruit chāt is very nourishing and appetising. We used to make it every afternoon after the meal especially in the guava season. It is nice to make the fruit chāt with several varieties of fruit but one can make it with as few as two different fruits. You will find this fruit chāt to be of medium hotness.

Ingredients:	Metric	Imperial	American
Apple, washed and cut into			
2.5 cm / 1" pieces	*100 g*	*4 oz*	*4 oz*
Pear, washed and cut into			
2.5 cm / 1" pieces	*100 g*	*4 oz*	*4 oz*
Guavas washed and cut into			
2.5 cm / 1" pieces	*100 g*	*4 oz*	*4 oz*
Grapes (preferably seedless)	*100 g*	*4 oz*	*4 oz*
Banana	*3*	*3*	*3*
Lemon juice	*30 ml*	*2 tbsp*	*2 tbsp*
Sugar	*15 ml*	*1 tbsp*	*1 tbsp*
Garam masala	*1.2 ml*	*¼ tsp*	*¼ tsp*
Ground red chilli	*0.8 ml*	*⅛ tsp*	*⅛ tsp*
Salt to taste			

Preparation time: 10 minutes

Place all the above ingredients in a bowl. Mix well and serve it cold. Other fruits which can be used for chāt are pineapple, orange, papaya, apricot, peach and melon etc.

Serving Suggestion:

Serve after a meal. It is an exciting way of eating fresh fruits.

Today I have again decided to combine a selection of vegetarian and non-vegetarian dishes. Chicken with cream, nuts and spices is just superb. Chola dal cooked in this East Indian style gives it a flavour unique to itself. Bharta cooked in this north Indian style is also irresistible. Perhaps you can make a night of it and cook the aubergine in the hot ashes of a bonfire.

 Malai Murgi
(Creamed Chicken)

Serves: 6

This creamed chicken dish is a treasure from the Indian cuisine.
It is an oriental delight for you and your guest. You will find this
dish to be of medium hotness.

Ingredients:	Metric	Imperial	American
Chicken, skinned, washed and cut into 16 pieces	1.4 kg	3 lb	3 lb
Ghee or oil	75 ml	5 tbsp	5 tbsp
Large garlic clove, crushed	4	4	4
Fresh ginger, finely chopped	4 cm	1½ "	1½ "
Medium onion, finely chopped	3	3	3
*Cloves	4	4	4 ½ tsp
*Peppercorns	4	4	4 ½ tsp
Bay leaves	3	3	3
*Cinnamon stick	2.5 cm	1"	1" ½ tsp
*Black cardamom	1	1	1 ½ tsp
Garam masala	5 ml	1 tsp	1 tsp
Ground roasted cumin	5 ml	1 tsp	1 tsp
Ground red chilli	2.5 ml	½ tsp	½ tsp
Ground turmeric	2.5 ml	½ tsp	½ tsp
Ground nutmeg	1.5 ml	¼ tsp	¼ tsp
Ground mace	1.5 ml	¼ tsp	¼ tsp
Salt to taste			½ tsp
Milk	300 ml	½ pt	1¼ cups
Raisins	150 g	5 oz	5 oz
Almonds, blanched and cut in halves lengthwise	75 g	3 oz	3 oz
Cashewnuts, cut in halves lengthwise	75 g	3 oz	3 oz
Pistachios, cut in halves lengthwise	25 g	1 oz	1 oz

Malai Murgi
(Creamed Chicken)

DAY 17

Ingredients:	Metric	Imperial	American
~~Ground green cardamom~~	2.5 ml	$^{1}/_{2}$ tsp	$^{1}/_{2}$ tsp
~~Cream (single)~~ plain yogurt	284 ml	10 fl oz	~~1 $^{1}/_{4}$~~ cups
To Garnish:			
Garam masala	2.5 ml	$^{1}/_{2}$ tsp	$^{1}/_{2}$ tsp
Green coriander leaves, finely chopped	15 ml	1 tbsp	1 tbsp
Small green chilli, finely chopped	1	1	1

Cooking Time: 40 minutes

1 Heat the ghee in a large heavy-bottomed saucepan. Put in the onion, garlic, ginger, bay leaves, cloves, cinnamon, black cardamom and peppercorns and fry gently until golden brown.

2 Add the chicken pieces and fry for about 10 minutes until lightly golden brown on all sides.

3 Stir in garam masala, roasted cumin, red chilli, turmeric, nutmeg, mace, salt and milk.

4 Bring it to the boil. Reduce the heat to medium low and cover the pan. Cook for 15 minutes, stirring occasionally.

5 Open the lid and add the chopped cashewnuts, almonds and pistachios, raisins and the cardamom and fry on medium heat until all the liquid has been absorbed and the ghee appears on the top of the mixture and the chicken is tender.

6 Reduce the heat to low and pour in the cream. Allow to simmer for 2 minutes.

7 Sprinkle over the garnish.

Serving Suggestion:

Serve hot with rice, puri, stuffed aubergine and salad.

Chola Dal
(Split yellow peas: East India - Bengali Style)

DAY 17

Serves: 4-6

Chola dal (gram dal or split yellow peas) is very popular among all Indians although the way of cooking is slightly different in various parts of India. I think that the Bengali style of this cooked lentil is absolutely delicious. It gives an unique sweet and sour taste.

Ingredients:	Metric	Imperial	American
Gram dal, cleaned, washed and soaked for an hour	250 g	9 oz	9 oz
Turmeric	2.5 ml	1/2 tsp	1/2 tsp
Water	1.7 l	3 pt	3 pt
Salt to taste			

Tarka:

Ingredients:	Metric	Imperial	American
Oil	45 ml	3 tbsp	3 tbsp
Bay leaves	2	2	2
Cumin	5 ml	1 tsp	1 tsp
Small onion, finely chopped	1	1	1
Fresh ginger, finely chopped	1.25 cm	1/2 "	1/2 "
Coconut, desiccated or fresh	50 g	2 oz	2 oz
Garam masala	2.5 ml	1/2 tsp	1/2 tsp
Ground red chilli	2.5 ml	1/2 tsp	1/2 tsp
Ground turmeric	1.5 ml	1/4 tsp	1/4 tsp
Small green chilli, finely chopped	1	1	1
Tamarind, extract pulp	25 g	1 oz	1 oz
Sugar	25 g	1 oz	1 oz

Real Indian Cookery a 21 Day Course

Chola Dal
(Split yellow peas:
East India - Bengali Style)

Ingredients:	To Garnish: Metric	Imperial	American
Green coriander leaves	15 ml	1 tbsp	1 tbsp
Garam masala	2.5 ml	¹/₂ tsp	¹/₂ tsp

Cooking Time: 1 hour

1 Put the dal in a large saucepan with the water, turmeric and the salt. Bring to the boil, skim off any scum and simmer on a medium heat for 50 minutes or until tender.
2 While the dal is cooking prepare the tarka. Heat the oil in a heavy bottomed saucepan, add the cumin seeds and brown them.
3 Add the onion, ginger and bay leaves and fry until light brown.
4 Stir in the coconut and fry it until golden brown.
5 Add the garam masala, red chilli, turmeric, green chilli, sugar and the tamarind pulp.
6 Bring the mixture to the boil and add it to the cooked lentils.
7 Stir and simmer for a further 10 minutes. The texture of the lentils should not be too thick. Sprinkle over the garnish before serving.

Serving Suggestion:
Serve hot with plain rice, okra, rayta and a meat or fish dish.

Bharta
(Mashed Aubergine - North Indian Style)

Serves: 4-6

For the bharta dish one needs large sized aubergines. In this recipe one needs to bake the aubergines in the oven. In India, most Indians still use wood or coal for cooking therefore normally people roast an aubergine under hot ashes - roasting this way adds extra taste to the dish. You will find this dish to be of medium hotness.

Ingredients:	Metric	Imperial	American
Large aubergine, baked or roasted at 200°C/ 400°F/ gas mark 6, peeled and mashed	500 g	18 oz	18 oz
Peas, frozen or fresh (shelled)	250 g	9 oz	2 1/3 cups
Oil	60 ml	4 tbsp	4 tbsp
Mustard seeds	2.5 ml	1/2 tsp	1/2 tsp
Cumin seeds	2.5 ml	1/2 tsp	1/2 tsp
Large garlic clove, crushed	3	3	3
Medium onion, finely chopped	2	2	2
Fresh ginger, finely chopped	2.5 cm	1"	1"
Ground coriander	30 ml	2 tbsp	2 tbsp
Ground red chilli	2.5 ml	1/2 tsp	1/2 tsp
Ground turmeric	1.25 ml	1/4 tsp	1/2 tsp
Garam masala	2.5ml	1/2 tsp	1/2 tsp
Tomatoes, tinned	400 g	14 oz	14 oz
Salt to taste			
To Garnish:			
Garam masala	2.5 ml	1/2 tsp	1/2 tsp
Green coriander leaves, chopped	15 ml	1 tbsp	1 tbsp
Small green chilli, chopped	1	1	1

Bharta
(Mashed Aubergine - North Indian Style)

Cooking Time: 30 minutes

1 Heat the oil in a heavy-bottomed saucepan.
2 Add the mustard seeds and fry them until they crackle.
3 Add the cumin seeds then the onion, garlic and the ginger and fry gently on a medium heat until they are lightly brown.
4 Stir in the mashed aubergine and cook for a further 2 minutes.
5 Then add the coriander, garam masala, red chilli, turmeric, salt and the tomatoes and cook until all the water has been absorbed and the oil appears on the top of the mixture.
6 Stir in the frozen peas and simmer for 5 minutes or until the peas are tender.
7 Sprinkle over the garnish before serving.

Serving Suggestions:

Serve hot with puri or chapati, rice, dal and a chicken dish.

DAY
18

Nearing the end of your 21 day course I shall now allow you to try a vegetarian delight. Green pepper stuffed with potatoes and raisins, cooked in a sweet and sour sauce is just wonderful. Aloo Kachori is another of those dishes suitable for all occasions and the picnic basket. They are quick and easy to make. Keema Kebab is a meat dish and can be eaten as a starter or as a dish with a meal.

Keema Kebab

Makes: 10

This is one of the delicious lamb mince meat dishes which can be served as a meal or at tea time. In this dish, mince is first cooked with lentils and spices and then ground (liquidised) to a very fine paste. The size of the kebab depends on individual choice. You will find this dish to be of medium hotness.

Preparing the meat paste:

Ingredients:	Metric	Imperial	American
Keema (lamb mince meat)	*250 g*	*9 oz*	*9 oz*
Gram dal (split yellow peas, soaked overnight in 500 ml / 18 fl oz water	*75 g*	*3 oz*	*3 oz*
Medium onion, coarsely chopped	*1*	*1*	*1*
Large garlic cloves, coarsely chopped	*1*	*1*	*1*
Fresh ginger, coarsely chopped	*2.5 cm*	*1"*	*1"*
Garam masala	*10 ml*	*2 tsp*	*2 tsp*
Ground red chilli	*2.5 ml*	*1/2 tsp*	*1/2 tsp*
Salt to taste			

1 Place all the above ingredients with the soaked dal, keema and 350 ml/ 12 fl oz/ 1 ½ cups water in a saucepan on a medium heat. Bring to the boil. Reduce the heat to medium-low and cook for 30 minutes or until the dal and meat are tender (if more water is needed, boil it first before adding).
2 Dry off any remaining liquid over a high heat.
3 When cold, place a little at a time in a blender and blend to make a smooth paste.
4 Divide into 10 equal portions.

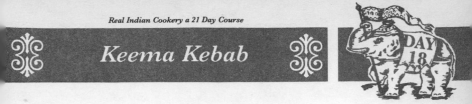

Keema Kebab

DAY 18

Preparing the filling:

Ingredients:	Metric	Imperial	American
Medium onion finely chopped	1	1	1
Small green chilli, finely chopped	1	1	1
Green coriander leaves, chopped	45 ml	3 tbsp	3 tbsp

Place the above ingredients on a plate and mix them thoroughly.
Divide the mixture into 10 equal portions.

Oil to Fry

Frying Time: 25 minutes

1 Place a few drops of oil on the palm of your hand.
2 Take a portion of meat paste, flatten it, place one portion of filling
   on it, bring the edges over to cover, roll tightly in a ball and
   flatten to 0.6 cm/ ¼ " thick. Make all the kebabs in the
   same manner.
3 Heat a flat frying pan on a medium heat. Smear with 15 ml/ 1
   tbsp oil, reduce the heat to medium-low and put in 4-6 kebabs.
4 Turn them over gently after 2 minutes. Pour in 15 ml/ 1 tbsp oil
   around the kebabs and fry the other side as well until golden
   brown. I don't turn the kebabs over more than 2-3 times.

Serving Suggestion:

Serve hot with a meal or at tea with chutney.

Aloo Katchori
(Potato Katchori)

Makes: 20

Aloo Katchori is an interesting variation of puri. It is a hearty bread and very popular in the U.P. (Uttar Pradesh). You will find this bread to be of medium hotness.

Preparing the dough:

Ingredients:	Metric	Imperial	American
Chapati flour, brown	*250 g*	*9 oz*	*2 1/4 cups*
Margarine	*25 g*	*1 oz*	*2 tbsp*
Natural yoghurt	*30 ml*	*2 tbsp*	*2 tbsp*
Tymol seeds (ajwain), cleaned	*2.5 ml*	*1/2 tsp*	*1/2 tsp*
Salt	*large pinch*	*large pinch*	*large pinch*
Water, luke warm	*100 ml*	*3 1/2 fl oz*	*6 1/2 tbsp*

Place the flour into a bowl. Add the margarine and mix thoroughly. Put in the rest of the ingredients and pour in the water to make a soft dough. Knead it for 5 minutes or until the dough is springy and satiny. Cover and leave for 30 minutes.

Preparing the filling:

Potatoes, boiled in jackets, peeled and mashed	*500 g*	*1 lb 2 oz*	*18 oz*
Green coriander leaves, chopped	*30 ml*	*2 tbsp*	*2 tbsp*
Small green chilli, finely chopped	*1*	*1*	*1*
Ground roasted cumin	*5 ml*	*1 tsp*	*1 tsp*
Garam masala	*2.5 ml*	*1/2 tsp*	*1/2 tsp*
Tymol seeds (ajwain), cleaned	*2.5 ml*	*1/2 tsp*	*1/2 tsp*
Ground red chilli	*1.5 ml*	*1/4 tsp*	*1/4 tsp*
Salt to taste			

Place the mashed potato, ground spices and the chopped ingredients in a bowl and mix them thoroughly. Divide the mixture into 20 equal portions.

Oil to Fry

Aloo Katchori
(Potato Katchori)

Cooking Time: 35 minutes

1 Heat the oil in a deep frying pan on medium heat. While the oil is heating, divide the dough into 20 equal portions.

2 Take a portion of dough, roll it into a ball with the palm of your hands and flatten it. Put a few drops of oil on the rolling board and roll into 5 cm/ 2" diameter circle.

3 Place one portion of filling on the dough and cover the filling by bringing the edges together.

4 Again flatten, put a few drops of oil on the rolling board and roll it into a round 4 mm/ $^1/_{10}$ " thick (with a rolling pin or by patting with your fingers).

5 Slip the aloo katchori gently into the hot oil from the edge of the pan. Gently press the aloo katchori with a slotted spoon all over and it will swell up a little.

6 Fry both sides light brown.

Serving Suggestions:

Serve hot at a meal with a vegetable dish, dahibara, chutney and pickle. The aloo kachories are ideal to be taken on a picnic.

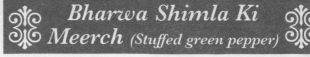

Bharwa Shimla Ki Meerch *(Stuffed green pepper)*

Serves: 4-6

The stuffed green pepper is one of my delicious party dishes. It looks very attractive on the dinner table. No doubt it takes a long time to prepare therefore I do two or three things together – like boiling the potatoes when I am cooking something else and preparing the sauce while the stuffed peppers are cooking. The potatoes and the sauce can be prepared the day before. This dish is of medium hotness.

Ingredients:	Metric	Imperial	American
Small green pepper, washed, cut a small cap around the stem with a pointed knife. Scoop out the seeds and mix in the filling	*500 g*	*1 lb 2 oz*	*18 oz*

Preparing the filling:

	Metric	Imperial	American
Potatoes, boiled in jackets, peeled and cut into small pieces	*1 kg*	*2 lb 4 oz*	*2 lb 4 oz*
Oil	*75 ml*	*5 tbsp*	*5 tbsp*
Cumin seeds	*5 ml*	*1 tsp*	*1 tsp*
Mustard seeds	*5 ml*	*1 tsp*	*1 tsp*
Ground coriander	*30 ml*	*2 tbsp*	*2 tbsp*
Ground roasted cumin	*5 ml*	*1 tsp*	*1 tsp*
Garam masala	*5 ml*	*1 tsp*	*1 tsp*
Ground red chilli	*2.5 ml*	*½ tsp*	*½ tsp*
Ground turmeric	*2.5 ml*	*½ tsp*	*½ tsp*
Salt to taste			
Raisins	*100 g*	*4 oz*	*½ cup*
Lemon juice	*30 ml*	*2 tbsp*	*2 tbsp*
Sugar	*10 ml*	*2 tsp*	*2 tsp*

Bharwa Shimla Ki Meerch *(Stuffed green pepper)*

DAY 18

Ingredients:	Metric	Imperial	American
Green coriander leaves, chopped	*15 ml*	*1 tbsp*	*1 tbsp*
Small green chilli, chopped	*1*	*1*	*1*

Cooking Time: 10 minutes

1 Heat the oil in a frying pan. Add the mustard seeds. When they start to crackle add the cumin seeds and the potato pieces and fry them on medium heat for 2-3 minutes.

2 Stir in the coriander, red chilli, turmeric, roasted cumin, salt and garam masala and fry for a further 2-3 minutes.

3 Add raisins, lemon juice, sugar, coriander leaves and green chilli and cook for one minute. Turn the heat off and set the pan on one side.

Preparing the sauce or paste:

Ingredients:	Metric	Imperial	American
Oil	*60 ml*	*4 tbsp*	*4 tbsp*
Mustard seeds	*2.5 ml*	*1/2 tsp*	*1/2 tsp*
Small onion, finely chopped	*1*	*1*	*1*
Large onion, coarsely chopped	*1*	*1*	*1*
Large garlic cloves, coarsely chopped	*3*	*3*	*3*
Fresh ginger, coarsely chopped	*1.3 cm*	*1/2 "*	*1/2 "*

Combine the large onion, garlic cloves and fresh ginger pieces in a blender with 60 ml/ 4 tbsp water and blend to make a fine paste.

Ground coriander	*10 ml*	*2 tsp*	*2 tsp*
Garam masala	*5 ml*	*1 tsp*	*1 tsp*
Ground red chilli	*2.5 ml*	*1/2 tsp*	*1/2 tsp*
Ground turmeric	*2.5 ml*	*1/2 tsp*	*1/2 tsp*
Tomatoes, tinned	*400 g*	*14 oz*	*14 oz*
Salt to taste			

DAY 18

Bharwa Shimla Ki Meerch *(Stuffed green pepper)*

Ingredients:	Metric	Imperial	American
Tamarind, thick pulp (see the recipe)	30 ml	2 tbsp	2 tbsp
Sugar	15 ml	1 tbsp	1 tbsp
To Garnish:			
Garam masala	2.5 ml	½ tsp	½ tsp
Green coriander leaves	15 ml	1 tbsp	1 tbsp
Small green chilli	1	1	1

Cooking Time: 35 minutes

1 Heat the oil in a large frying pan and add the mustard seeds.
2 When the seeds start to crackle add the chopped onion and fry until golden brown on medium heat.
3 Stir in the blended paste and fry again until golden brown.
4 Then add the coriander, garam masala, red chilli, turmeric, salt and the tomatoes and cook until the oil appears on the top of the mixture.
5 Stuff the peppers with the potato filling, place the tops back on. Place the stuffed peppers in the sauce, put the lid on the frying pan and cook on medium-low heat for 15 minutes, until the peppers are cooked. While cooking, baste with sauce and turn over three or four times.
6 Stir in the tamarind pulp and sugar and cook until all the liquid has been absorbed.

Garnish suggestion:

Place the stuffed peppers in a circle in a two inch deep serving dish, leaving some gaps between each pepper. Place the leftover potato mixture and paste (sauce) in each gap. Sprinkle over the garnish.

Serving Suggestion:

Serve hot with lentil, rice, puri or onion paratha and a chicken dish.

DAY
19

Today I will teach you to prepare
Chicken Tikka without a tandori
oven. If you like to eat this with sauce
see the Murgh Musallum recipe. For
vegetarians there is a nourishing and
delicious
carrot and peas dish. Today
you will be able to get the opportunity
to prepare another very popular
sweet. This is often prepared during
festivals in India.

DAY 19

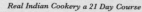

Chicken Tikka

Chicken Tikka is one of the most popular dishes of my cookery class. One can eat it as a starter or as a side dish with a meal. You will find this dish to be quite hot.

Ingredients:	Metric	Imperial	American
Chicken breast (skinned, boned, washed and cut into 4" pieces)	500 g	1 lb	1 lb
Yoghurt	150 g	5 oz	5 oz
Turmeric	2.5 ml	¹/₂ tsp	¹/₂ tsp
Red chilli	5 ml	1 tsp	1 tsp
Ground coriander	15 ml	1 tbsp	1 tbsp
Ground roasted cumin	15 ml	1 tbsp	1 tbsp
Lemon juice	15 ml	1 tbsp	1 tbsp
Sugar	15 ml	1 tbsp	1 tbsp
Garam masala	5 ml	1 tsp	1 tsp
Garlic, large cloves	4	4	4
Ginger	2.5 cm	1"	1"
Salt to taste			

1 Grind garlic and ginger with lemon juice and yoghurt to make a fine paste.
2 Add turmeric, red chilli, coriander, cumin, garam masala, salt and sugar to the paste and mix well.
3 Rub the ground paste into the chicken pieces and marinate them for 6 - 8 hours
4 Roast chicken pieces in over (200° C/ 400° F/ gas mark 6), for half an hour or until cooked.
5 Baste every so often with ghee.
6 Turn them every 10 minutes.
7 If you want to eat with sauce see the Murgh Musallum recipe on page 62.

Gajar - Matar Ki Sabji
(Carrot and Peas -
North Indian Style)

Serves: 4

This nourishing vegetable dish is cooked in every part of India but by different methods in different areas. In the West of India onion and garlic is avoided but lemon and sugar is added instead. You will find this dish to be of medium hotness.

Ingredients:	Metric	Imperial	American
Tender small carrots, washed and cut into 2.5 cm / 1" pieces	500 g	1 lb 2 oz	18 oz
Peas frozen (fresh, shelled)	250 g	9 oz	9 oz
Oil	60 ml	4 tbsp	4 tbsp
Mustard seeds	5 ml	1 tsp	1 tsp
Cumin seeds	5 ml	1 tsp	1 tsp
Large garlic cloves, crushed	2	2	2
Fresh ginger, finely chopped	1.2 cm	½ "	½ "
Medium onion, finely chopped	1	1	1
Ground coriander	10 ml	2 tsp	2 tsp
Garam masala	5 ml	1 tsp	1 tsp
Ground red chilli	2.5 ml	½ tsp	½ tsp
Ground turmeric	2.5 ml	½ tsp	½ tsp
Salt to taste			
Tomatoes, tinned	230 g	8 oz	8 oz
To Garnish:			
Garam masala	2.5 ml	½ tsp	½ tsp
Green coriander leaves, chopped	15 ml	1 tbsp	1 tbsp
Small green chilli, chopped	1	1	1

Gajar - Matar Ki Sabji
(Carrot and Peas - North Indian Style)

DAY 19

Cooking Time: 30 minutes

1 Heat the oil in a large heavy-bottomed saucepan.
2 Add the mustard seeds and when they start crackling brown the cumin seeds.
3 Put in the onion, garlic and the ginger and fry gently on medium heat until golden brown.
4 Stir in the coriander, garam masala, red chilli, turmeric and salt and then the tomatoes and the carrots.
5 Close the lid reduce the heat to medium - low and cook for 10 minutes or until carrot pieces are slightly tender, stirring occasionally.
6 Mix in the peas and cook for a further few minutes until the peas are tender and the oil appears on the surface of the mixture.
7 Increase the heat and dry off any remaining water.
8 Sprinkle over the garnish before serving.

Serving Suggestions:
Serve hot with dal, rice, puri, rayta and a fish dish.

Gujiya

Makes: 16

This is an elegant sweet snack which is specially prepared by most Hindus to celebrate the auspicious festival of Deepawali (the festival of lights and fireworks) and Holi (the festival of colour).

Preparing the dough:

Ingredients:	Metric	Imperial	American
Plain flour	125 g	4 oz	1 cup
Margarine	25 g	1 oz	2 tbsp
Water, luke warm	50 ml	2 fl oz	1/4 cup

Rub the margarine into the four. Pour in the water and knead for 2 minutes or until the dough is soft, springy and satiny. Cover and leave for 30 minutes.

Preparing the filling:

Ingredients:	Metric	Imperial	American
Ghee	7.5 ml	1 1/2 tsp	1 1/2 tsp
Sultanas	50 g	2 oz	2 oz
Almonds, blanched and finely chopped	25 g	1 oz	1 oz
Pistachios, finely chopped	15 g	1/2 oz	1/2 oz
Khoya (see miscellaneous recipe page 21), made from full cream milk powder	75 g	3 oz	3 oz
Sugar	75 g	3 oz	3 oz
Ground green cardamom	2.5 ml	1/2 tsp	1/2 tsp
Saffron (soaked in 15 ml/ 1 tbsp warm milk)	1.5 ml	1/4 tsp	1/4 tsp

1   Heat the ghee in a saucepan on medium low heat and fry the chopped nuts and sultanas for 2 minutes.

Gujiya

2 Mix in the khoya, sugar, cardamom and the saffron and cook for a further 3 minutes, stirring continuously. Turn the heat off. Set the pan on one side to cool.

Preparing the Gujiya:
Ghee and oil mixture (equal quantities) to fry.

Cooking Time: 1 hour

1 Heat the fat in a deep frying pan on medium - low heat. While the fat is heating, divide the dough and the filling into 16 equal portions.
2 Take a portion of dough and roll into a ball on the palm of your hands, flatten it and thinly roll it about 11.5 cm/ 4½" round in diameter (do not use flour or oil for rolling).
3 Place one portion of filling on a round of dough.
4 Lift one side gently and fold over (giving half moon shape), press both the edges to seal and pinch with your fingers to give an attractive pattern.
5 Slip the gujiya gently into the hot fat from the edge of the pan. Make another gujiya and add to the fat, turn them over only 3 - 4 times.
6 Fry 4 - 5 gujiya together until lightly golden brown on all sides. Keep on making them, do not keep them on the rolling board after making but cook immediately. Leave them to cool on a cooling tray.

Serving Suggestion:
Serve hot or cold after a meal or at tea with dalmod and pakora.

Today is a perfect day for fish lovers. English fish flakes very easily therefore I have adapted the recipe slightly. Fish dishes are very popular in Bengal and usually people eat fish daily. Red beans are cooked in Punjab very regularly, more so than in any other part of India. Puri Walé Aloo is very simple to prepare and this curry is absolutely delicious.

Puri Walé Aloo
(Potato Curry)

Serves: 4

This is a most simple and delicious dish. You will find this dish to be medium hot.

Ingredients:	Metric	Imperial	American
Potatoes, boiled in jackets, peeled and cut into 0.6 cm/ ¼ " pieces	500 g	1 lb 2 oz	18 oz
Oil or ghee	60 ml	4 tbsp	4 tbsp
Mustard seeds	2.5 ml	½ tsp	½ tsp
Cumin seeds	2.5 ml	½ tsp	½ tsp
Ground coriander	5 ml	1 tsp	1 tsp
Ground roasted cumin	5 ml	1 tsp	1 tsp
Garam masala	2.5 ml	½ tsp	½ tsp
Ground red chilli	2.5 ml	½ tsp	½ tsp
Ground turmeric	2.5 ml	½ tsp	½ tsp
Salt to taste			
Tomatoes, tinned	400 g	14 fl oz	14 fl oz
Water	150 ml	¼ pt	⅔ cup
Lemon juice	15 ml	1 tbsp	1 tbsp

	To Garnish:		
Ingredients:	Metric	Imperial	American
Garam masala	2.5 ml	½ tsp	½ tsp
Green coriander leaves, chopped	15 ml	1 tbsp	1 tbsp
Small green chilli, chopped	1	1	1

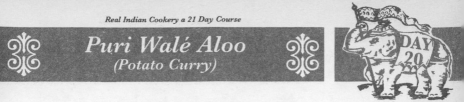

Puri Walé Aloo
(Potato Curry)

DAY 20

Cooking Time: 20 minutes

1 Heat the oil in a heavy-bottomed saucepan. Add the mustard seeds and when they start crackling add the cumin seeds and fry until they are golden brown.

2 Mix in the potato pieces and fry them light brown.

3 Stir in the ground coriander, roasted cumin, garam masala, red chilli, turmeric, salt and tomatoes and cook until all the liquid has been absorbed.

4 Pour in the water and bring to boil. Reduce the heat to low and simmer it for 2 minutes.

5 Add the lemon juice.

6 Sprinkle over the garnish before serving.

Serving Suggestions:

Serve hot with puries, jalebi, lasi and pickle at breakfast or at any meal.

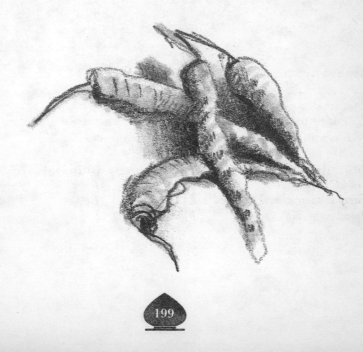

Rajma
(Red beans - North Indian - Punjabi Style)

Serves: 4-6

Red beans and black eyed beans are one of the best and richest sources of protein especially for vegetarians. They are very tasty and most Punjabies cook them at least once a week. Sometimes I add a handful of whole black urud lentil as well before soaking. This dish is of medium hotness.

Ingredients:	Metric	Imperial	American
Rajma, cleaned and soaked overnight	250 g	9 oz	9 oz
Salt to taste			
Ghee or oil	90 ml	6 tbsp	6 tbsp
Small onion, finely chopped	1	1	1
*Cloves	4	4	4
*Peppercorns	4	4	4
Bay leaves	2	2	2
*Cinnamon stick	1.2 cm	1/2 "	1/2 "
*Black cardamom	1	1	1
Large garlic cloves, chopped	3	3	3
Fresh ginger, chopped	2.5 cm	1"	1"
Medium onion, coarsely chopped	1	1	1

Combine the garlic, ginger and onion in a blender with 45 ml / 3 tbsp water and blend to make a smooth paste.

Ingredients:	Metric	Imperial	American
Ground coriander	5 ml	1 tsp	1 tsp
Ground roasted cumin	5 ml	1 tsp	1 tsp
Garam masala	2.5 ml	1/2 tsp	1/2 tsp
Ground red chilli	2.5 ml	1/2 tsp	1/2 tsp
Ground turmeric	2.5 ml	1/2 tsp	1/2 tsp
Salt to taste			

Rajma
(Red beans - North Indian - Punjabi Style)

DAY 20

Ingredients:	Metric	Imperial	American
Tomatoes, tinned	150 g	5 oz	$^3/_1$ cup
Water	2.8 l	5 pt	12 cups
	To Garnish:		
Garam masala	2.5 ml	$^1/_2$ tsp	$^1/_2$ tsp
Green coriander leaves, chopped	15 ml	1 tbsp	1 tbsp
Small green chilli, chopped	1	1	1

Cooking Time: 1 hour 35 minutes

Place the soaked rajma, salt and the water in a large saucepan (if the pan is not large enough then add boiled water as needed) on medium heat. Bring to the boil, reduce the heat to medium-low, close the lid and cook for 1 hour 20 minutes or until the rajma are tender.

Prepare the sauce while the rajma are cooking:

1. Heat the ghee in a large heavy - bottomed saucepan on a medium heat; and fry the finely chopped onion, bay leaves, cloves, peppercorns, cinnamon, cardamom and until golden brown.
2. Put in the blended paste and fry for a further few minutes until golden brown.
3. Stir in garam masala, coriander, red chilli, turmeric, roasted cumin, salt and then the tomatoes and cook until all the liquid has been absorbed and the ghee appears on the surface of the mixture.
4. Add the cooked rajma and cook for a further 15 minutes or until the required thickness of sauce is obtained.
5. Sprinkle over the garnish before serving.

Serving Suggestion:
Serve hot with plain rice, chapati, cauliflower, rayta and a chicken dish.

Machli Ki Sabji
(Fish Curry)

Serves: 4-6

This fish dish is very delicious and easy to make. The spices add
flavour to the bland fish. Take care when frying the fish pieces.
Turn them over 2 or 3 times only.

Preparing the fish pieces:

Ingredients:	Metric	Imperial	American
Fish (cod or haddock), boned, cut into 4 cm/ 1 ¹/₂ " pieces and washed	500 g	1 lb 2 oz	18 oz
Large garlic cloves, chopped	4	4	4
Medium onion, cut into large pieces	2	2	2
Fresh ginger, chopped	2.5 cm	1"	1"
Vinegar	50 ml	2 fl oz	3 ¹/₂ tbsp

Combine the last four ingredients in a blender and blend to make a
fine paste. Divide the paste into two portions. Marinate the fish pieces
in one of the ground paste portions for one hour. Set the other
portion to one side for the sauce.

Oil to fry

Frying Time: 30 minutes

1 Heat 45 ml/ 3 tbsp oil in a flat frying pan. Place in half of the
marinated fish pieces and fry on a medium heat for 15 minutes
or until light brown.
2 Turn them over 2 - 3 times only. Take them out with a slotted
spoon and place them on the serving dish. Do the same with
the rest of the fish.

Preparing the sauce:

Prepare the sauce while the fish is marinating

Oil	60 ml	4 tbsp	4 tbsp
Mustard seeds	5 ml	1 tsp	1 tsp

Machli Ki Sabji
(Fish Curry)

Ingredients:	Metric	Imperial	American
Small onion, finely chopped	1	1	1
*Cloves	4	4	4
*Peppercorns	4	4	4
Bay leaves	2	2	2
*Black cardamom	1	1	1
*Cinnamon stick	1.2 cm	½ "	½ "
Blended paste			
Garam masala	5 ml	1 tsp	1 tsp
Ground coriander	5 ml	1 tsp	1 tsp
Ground roasted cumin	5 ml	1 tsp	1 tsp
Ground turmeric	5 ml	1 tsp	1 tsp
Ground red chilli	2.5 ml	½ tsp	½ tsp
Salt to taste			
Tomatoes, tinned	230 g	8 oz	8 oz
Yoghurt	150 g	5 oz	5 oz
Lemon	15 ml	1 tbsp	1 tbsp
Sugar	15 ml	1 tbsp	1 tbsp
Water	200 ml	7 fl oz	7 fl oz

To garnish:

	Metric	Imperial	American
Garam masala	2.5 ml	½ tsp	½ tsp
Green coriander leaves, chopped	15 ml	1 tbsp	1 tbsp
Small green chilli, chopped finely	1	1	1

Cooking Time: 30 minutes

1 Heat the oil in a large heavy-bottomed saucepan on medium heat.
   Add the mustard seeds and when they start crackling fry the
   chopped onion, bay leaves, cloves, peppercorns, black
   cardamom, cinnamon stick until golden brown.

Machli Ki Sabji
(Fish Curry)

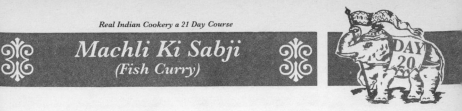

DAY 20

2 Mix in the blended paste and fry for a further few minutes until golden brown.

3 Stir in the garam masala, roasted cumin ,coriander, turmeric, red chilli, salt and the tomatoes and cook until all the liquid has been absorbed.

4 Put in the yoghurt and cook again until all the liquid is absorbed and the oil appears on the surface of the mixture. Add lemon and sugar and cook for a further 2 minutes. Pour the sauce over the fried fish pieces and sprinkle over the garnish before serving.

Serving Suggestion:
Serve hot with chapati, rice, dal, rayta and bean - potato.

To complete your 21 day schedule of Indian Cookery I shall introduce you to a new and original meat dish. Dry Meat Massala is very popular amongst all meat lovers. For vegetarians stuffed tomatoes are just the thing for you. Vegetarian Biriyani can also be prepared today. The resulting flavour of the above dishes gives credit to the cook if they are cooked well. I'll end a hard days work with just one more dish - Rasgulla. Many Asians find this dish difficult to prepare, however if you follow the recipe carefully you will achieve good results. Good luck and happy cooking!

Sukha Masalé Wala Gosht (Dry Meat Masala)

Serves: 4-6

This is a popular dish from the Northern cuisine of India. In dry meat masala, meat is cooked separately and then matured in spices and onion etc. It is full of flavour. You will find this dish quite hot.

Ingredients:	Metric	Imperial	American
Meat (lamb shoulder, boneless), cut into 2.5 cm /1" pieces, trimmed fat and washed	500 g	1 lb 2 oz	18 oz
Ghee or oil	75 ml	5 tbsp	5 tbsp
Onion seeds	5 ml	1 tsp	1 tsp
Sesame seeds	5 ml	1 tsp	1 tsp
Bay leaves	4	4	4
Large garlic cloves, crushed	3	3	3
Fresh ginger, finely chopped	2.5 cm	1"	1"
Medium onion, finely chopped	2	2	2
Ground almond powder	15 ml	1 tbsp	1 tbsp
Ground coriander	15 ml	1 tbsp	1 tbsp
Ground roasted cumin	5 ml	1 tsp	1 tsp
Garam masala	5 ml	1 tsp	1 tsp
Ground red chilli	2.5 ml	1/2 tsp	1/2 tsp
Ground turmeric	2.5 ml	1/2 tsp	1/2 tsp
Ground mace	1.5 ml	1/4 tsp	1/4 tsp
Ground nutmeg	1.5 ml	1/4 tsp	1/4 tsp
Salt to taste			

To Garnish:

Garam masala	2.5 ml	1/2 tsp	1/2 tsp
Green coriander leaves, chopped	15 ml	1 tbsp	1 tbsp
Small green chilli, chopped	1	1	1

Sukha Masalé Wala Gosht (Dry Meat Masala)

Cooking Time: 45 minutes

1 Place the meat pieces with 400 ml/ 14 fl oz/ 2 cups of water into a saucepan. Bring to boil. Reduce the heat to medium-low, close the lid and cook for 30 minutes.

2 While the meat is cooking, heat the ghee in a heavy-bottomed saucepan on medium heat.

3 Add the onion seeds and brown them for 5 seconds.

4 Put in the sesame seeds and then the onion, garlic, bay leaves and ginger and fry them until golden brown.

5 Stir in the ground almond, coriander, roasted cumin, garam masala, red chilli, turmeric, mace, nutmeg and salt. (Turn the heat off and set to one side assuring all the meat is cooked).

6 Add the cooked meat pieces in the saucepan and cook until all the liquid has been absorbed.

7 Pour in 50 ml/ 2 fl oz/3$^{1}/_{2}$ tbsp water and cook again until all the water is absorbed and the ghee appears on the surface of the mixture.

8 Repeat this two or three times (add a small quantities of water only, this will not only help to fry nicely but will stop the spitting and splashing as well).

9 When the meat is tender, turn the heat off, sprinkle over the garnish before serving.

Serving Suggestion:
Serve hot with puri, dal, rayta and a kofta dish.

Bharwa Tomatar
(Stuffed Tomato)

Serves: 4-6

Stuffed tomato is a very attractive party side dish. For this dish one needs firm tomatoes of equal size.

Ingredients:	Metric	Imperial	American
Meat firm tomatoes, slice off the top, about ¼ cm ⅛ " thick skins and carefully scoop out the pulp. Turn them over and place on a plate. Do not throw away the pulp.	500 g	1 lb 2 oz	18 oz
Potatoes, boiled in jackets, peeled and cut into tiny pieces	500 g	1 lb 2 oz	18 oz
Mixed vegetables frozen or fresh (boiled)	250 g	9 oz	9 oz
Oil	75 ml	5 tbsp	5 tbsp
Mustard seeds	5 ml	1 tsp	1 tsp
Garam masala	5 ml	1 tsp	1 tsp
Ground coriander	5 ml	1 tsp	1 tsp
Ground roasted cumin	5 ml	1 tsp	1 tsp
Ground red chilli	2.5 ml	½ tsp	½ tsp
Ground turmeric	2.5 ml	½ tsp	½ tsp
Salt to taste			
Raisins	100 g	4 oz	⅔ cup
Green coriander leaves, chopped	30 ml	2 tbsp	2 tbsp
Small green chilli	1	1	1
Oil for frying			

Bharwa Tomatar
(Stuffed Tomato)

Cooking Time: 25 minutes

1　Heat the oil in a flat frying pan on medium heat. Add the mustard seeds and when they start crackling fry the potato pieces on a medium - low heat for 5 minutes or until they are light golden brown.

2　Stir in the garam masala, coriander, roasted cumin, turmeric, salt, red chilli, and then the mixed vegetables and the tomato pulp and cook for 7 minutes.

3　Put in the raisins and stir well. Mix in the chopped coriander leaves and green chilli and turn the heat off.

4　Stuff the tomatoes with the potato mixture. Replace the top.

5　Heat 45 ml/ 3 tbsp oil in a frying pan on a medium - low heat. Place all the stuffed tomatoes in the frying pan and fry them for 2 minutes. Gently turn them over and fry for a further minute.

Garnish Suggestion:

Place one cooked tomato in the centre of the serving dish and arrange the rest of the tomatoes around it in a circle. Spread the left-over filling around the tomatoes.

Serving Suggestion:

Serve hot with chutney, pulao, puri, dal, yoghurt and a chicken dish.

Rasgulla

Makes: 14

Rasgulla is a famous and delicious sweet dish from the Bengal. It is white coloured, light, soft and juicy, made from paneer (Indian style cheese). Bengali sweets are very popular all over India.

Ingredients:	Metric	Imperial	American
Milk, silver top	*1.1 l*	*2 pt*	*4½ cups*
Lemon juice	*45 ml*	*3 tbsp*	*3 tbsp*

1 Heat the milk, just as it begins to boil add the lemon juice (to separate the milk). Turn the heat off and leave for 2 minutes.
2 Strain the curd from the whey using a muslin cloth (keeping the whey for cooking lentil or vegetables).
3 Wash the curd (paneer) with cold water to remove any remaining fat from it.
4 Squeeze out all the water and press under a heavy object (a large saucepan filled with water) on top of an upturned plate for 30 minutes.

Ingredients:	Metric	Imperial	American
Sugar	*350 g*	*12 oz*	*1½ cups*
Water	*2.3 l*	*4 pt*	*9 cups*
Semolina	*10 ml*	*2 tsp*	*2 tsp*
Essence, Gulab or Kevera water	*5 ml*	*1 tsp*	*1 tsp*

Cooking Time: 1 hour and 20 minutes

1 Place the water and sugar in a large saucepan for boiling (if you do not have a large saucepan, boil the sugar in less water and add boiling water to the pan as needed until you have made up to the 2.3 lt/ 4 pt required) on medium heat.

Rasgulla

2 While the syrup is boiling, mix the paneer and the semolina in a bowl with the palm of your hand until it is soft and springy.

3 Divide into 11 equal portions and in the palm of your hands roll into tight balls. Add the paneer balls to the boiling syrup and cook for 1 hour and until the syrup is reduced to a quarter of the volume.

4 Remove from the heat and cool. When very cold put it in a bowl with the syrup. Keep it in a refrigerator for 3 - 4 hours before serving.

5 Stir in the essence just before serving.

Serving Suggestion:

Serve cold at tea with samosa and pakora or after the meal as a dessert.

Vegetable Biryani

Serves: 4-6

Due to my experimental nature with food this delightful dish came into existence. Yellow corn with paneer in a dark coloured sauce and layers of nutty saffron rice makes it very attractive. Its aroma increases the appetite.

Preparing the vegetable layer:

Ingredients:	Metric	Imperial	American
Corn frozen loose (or any other vegetable)	250 g	9 oz	9 oz
Paneer (see miscellaneous recipe page 22), cut into 1.2 cm ¹/₂ " square pieces	1.1 l	2 pt	2 pt
Oil or ghee	60 ml	4 tbsp	4 tbsp
Cumin seeds	2.5 ml	¹/₂ tsp	¹/₂ tsp
Large garlic cloves, crushed	2	2	2
Fresh ginger, finely chopped	1.2 cm	¹/₂ "	¹/₂ "
Medium onion, finely chopped	1	1	1
Coconut desiccated (or fresh - grated)	60 ml	4 tbsp	4 tbsp
Garam masala	5 ml	1 tsp	1 tsp
Ground coriander	5 ml	1 tsp	1 tsp
Ground roasted cumin	5 ml	1 tsp	1 tsp
Ground red chilli	2.5 ml	¹/₂ tsp	¹/₂ tsp
Ground turmeric	2.5 ml	¹/₂ tsp	¹/₂ tsp
Salt to taste			
Tomatoes, tinned	400 g	14 oz	14 oz
Green coriander leaves, chopped	30 ml	2 tbsp	2 tbsp
Lemon juice	30 ml	2 tbsp	2 tbsp
Mint leaves, chopped	15 ml	1 tbsp	1 tbsp

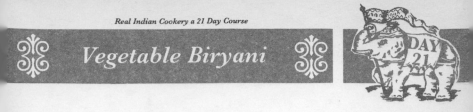

Vegetable Biryani

DAY 21

Cooking Time: 25 minutes

1 Heat the oil in a heavy-bottomed large saucepan on medium heat, and brown the cumin seeds.
2 Add the onion, garlic and the ginger and fry until golden brown.
3 Put in the coconut and fry for a further 2 minutes.
4 Stir in red chilli, garam masala, coriander, cumin, turmeric, salt and then the tomatoes, corn and the paneer. Cook until all the liquid has been absorbed.
5 Mix in the lemon juice, coriander and mint leaves thoroughly. Set the pan on one side (re-heat before placing in layers with the rice). Prepare the rice while the corn is cooking.

Preparing the rice layer:

Ingredients:	Metric	Imperial	American
Rice (Patna or basmati), cleaned, washed and drained	250 g	9 oz	2 cups
Ghee	90 ml	6 tbsp	6 tbsp
Cumin seeds	5 ml	1 tsp	1 tsp
Medium onion, thinly sliced	1	1	1
Cloves	4	4	4
Peppercorns	4	4	4
Cinnamon stick	2.5 cm	1"	1"
Bay leaves	2	2	2
Black cardamom	1	1	1
Garam masala	5 ml	1 tsp	1 tsp
Ground roasted cumin	5 ml	1 tsp	1 tsp
Salt to taste			
Raisins	100 g	4 oz	2/3 cup
Cashewnuts, cut in halves lengthwise	50 g	2 oz	1/3 cup

215

DAY 21

Vegetable Biryani

Ingredients:	Metric	Imperial	American
Water	500 ml	18 fl oz	4 cups

Cooking Time: 20 minutes

1 Heat the ghee in a large heavy-bottomed saucepan and brown the cumin seeds.
2 Add the onion, bay leaves, cloves, peppercorns, black cardamom, cinnamon and fry until golden brown.
3 Mix in the rice and fry for 2 minutes.
4 Stir in the cumin, garam masala, salt and then the raisins, cashewnuts and the water.
5 Bring to the boil, reduce the heat to low, close the lid and cook for 15 minutes.

Layering the rice and the vegetables:

Ingredients:	Metric	Imperial	American
Milk, warm	50 ml	2 fl oz	2 fl oz
Saffron	2.5 ml	1/2 tsp	1/2 tsp

Place the saffron in the warm milk.

1 Take a heavy-bottomed saucepan and place alternate layers of vegetables and rice. Repeat until you have used all the mixture.
2 Pour the saffron milk over the vegetables and layers of rice.
3 Close the lid and cook on a low heat for a further 5 minutes.
4 Before serving place a serving dish on the saucepan and carefully turn over. Tap a little all over the saucepan with a spoon.
5 Gently lift the saucepan, making sure all the biryani is in the serving dish.

Serving Suggestion:

Serve hot with rayta, salad and matar-aloo.

I am sure that this book is one of the most suitable books for everyone's kitchen shelf. The inception of this book dates back to fourteen years ago when I started teaching cookery during the evenings at various centres in Cambridgeshire.

Week after week I heard my students say that they had just cooked the best dish of their lives which was very encouraging and motivated me enough to put my oriental culinary expertise onto paper.

This book caters for all occasions i.e. wedding, parties, daily meals, breakfast, tea snacks, starters, drinks and chāts. It also contains popular mouthwatering dishes from all over India - North, South, East and West. I have included many popular breads, lentils, rice, meat, chicken, fish, vegetables, drinks, yoghurt, chutney and papadom, and have taken care to ensure that there is plenty for vegetarians as well as non-vegetarians.

With practice the variety enables one to be in a position to host a banquet! A bonus point is that you'll be able to prepare things according to your own taste rather than what a restaurant offers you. Food cooked at home with freshly ground spices fills your dining-room with aroma, making you and your guest even more hungry.

A few points to remember, 13/16
Aloo, Goghi and Gosht, 110/111
Aloo Katchori, 182/183
Aloo Ki Tikiya, 162/163
Aloo Paratha, 132/133
Balushahi, 104/105
Bharta, 176/177
Bharwa Shimla Ki Meerch, 184/186
Bharwa Tomatar, 210/211
Bhindi, Fried or Okra, 157
Bhutoora, 58/59
Biryani: Chicken Mughlai, 120/122
   Vegetable, 214/216
Bombay Mix, 100/102
Breads: Aloo Katchori, 182/183
   Bhutoora, 58/59
   Chapati, 40
   Dosa, 88/89
   Idli, 150
   Onion Paratha, 108
   Puri, 32/33
   Roghni Nan, 66/67
   Rolls, Stuffed, 72/73
Carrot and Peas - North Indian
   Style, 192/193
Carrot Halwa, 143
Chapati, 40
Chāt: Papri, 166/167
   Fruit Chāt, 168
Chicken Curry, 138/139
Chicken: Mughlai Biryani, 120/122
   Tikka, 190
   Whole with Nuts, Minced Lamb
      and Rice, 62/65
Chickpeas with Tamarind, 56/57
Chocolate and Coconut Barfi, 34/35
Chola Dal, 174/175

Chutney: Tamarind, 48/49
   Dhaniya, 76
   Coconut, 90/91
Coconut and Chocolate Barfi, 34/35
Coconut Chutney, 90/91
Creamed Chicken, 172/173
Curry: Chicken, 138/139
   Egg, 30/31
   Fish, 202/204
   Potato, 198/199
   Potato, Cauliflower and Meat,
      110/111
Dal: Chola, 174/175
   Urud Ki Sukhi, 114/115
Dalmod, 100/102
Dhandai, 134/135
Dhaniya Chutney, 76
Dhansank, 154/156
Dosa, 88/89
Drinks: Dhandai, 134/135
   Falooda, 85
   Lassi, 68
Dry Meat Masala, 208/209
Egg Curry, 30/31
Falooda, 85
Fenugreek Leaves, 38/39
Fish Curry, 202/204
Fried Bhindi or Okra, 157
Fried Fish, 92/93
Fruit Chāt, 168
Gajar Ka Halwa, 143
Gajar - Matar Ki Sabji, 192/193
Garam Masala, 19
Ghee, 20
Gol Guppa, 164/165
Gujiya, 194/195
Gulab Jamun, 74/75

Index

Ice-cream: Kulfi, 84
 Falooda, garnish for: 85
Idli, 150
Indian Cheese, 22
Introduction, 11/12
Jalebi, 50/51
Keema Kebab, 180/181
Khatéwalé Kabuli Chunna, 56/57
Khoya: Traditional, 21
 Quick way of making, 21
Korma: Mixed Vegetable, 112/113
Kulfi, 84
Lady's Finger, North Indian
 Style, 157
Lamb: Keema Kebab, 180/181
 Pork or Lamb Vindaloo, 80/81
 Rogan Josh, 146/147
 Sindhi Style Meat, 38/39
Lassi, 68
Machli Ki Sabji, 202/204
Malai Murgi, 172/173
Mashed Aubergine - North
 Indian Style, 176/177
Matar Paneer, 118/119
Miscellaneous: 18/27
 Garam Masala, 19
 Ghee, 20
 Khoya, 21
 Paneer, 22
 Potatoes Boiled in their
  Jackets, 23
 Roasted Cumin, 24
 Sambar Masala, 25
 Tamarind Pulp, 26
 Yoghurt, 27
Mixed Vegetable Korma, 112/113
Nuts: Dalmod, 100/102

Stuffed Murgh Masalam, 62/65
Vegetable Pulao with Nuts,
 94/95
Okra, Fried Bhindi or, 157
Onion and Spinach, 98/99
Onion Paratha, 108/109
Pakora, 98/99
Paneer, 22
Papri, 166/167
Peas and Indian Cheese, 118/119
Pork or Lamb Vindaloo, 80/81
Potatoes Boiled in Jackets, 23
Potato, Cauliflower and Meat
 Curry, 110/111
Potato Katchori, 182/183
Potato Paratha, 132/133
Potato Patties, North Indian
 Style, 162/163
Pulao: Prawn, 54/55
 Vegetable with Nuts, 94/95
Puri, 32/33
Puri Walé Aloo, 198/199
Rajma, 200/201
Rasgulla, 212/213
Rice: Chicken Mughlai
 Biryani, 120/122
 Dalmod, 100/102
 Prawn Pulao, 54/55
Roasted Cumin, 24
Rogan Josh (Kashmiri Style), 146/147
Roghni Nan, 66/67
Sabat Gobhi, 140/142
Sabat Moong Ki Hari Dal, 82/83
Sabudana Papar, 158/159
Sambar (South Indian Style), 148/149
Sambar Masala, 25
Sindhi Style Meat, 38/39

Index

South Indian Bread, 150
Split Yellow Peas (East India -
    Bengali style),174/175
Stuffed Bread Rolls, 72/73
Stuffed Green Peppers, 184/186
Stuffed Murgh Musallum 62/65
Stuffed Tomato, 210/211
Sukha Masalé Wala Gosht, 208/209
Sweet and Sour Prawns, 128/130
Sweetmeats: Balushahi, 104/105
    Coconut and Chocolate
        Barfi, 34/35
    Jalebi, 50/51
    Tirangi Barfi, 123/125
Tali Machli, 92/93
Tamarind: Pulp, 26
    Chutney, 48/49
    with Chickpeas, 56/57
Tapioca Papadum, 158/159
Three Coloured Barfi, 123/125
Tirangi Barfi, 123/125
Tomato, Cucumber and Onion
    Rayta, 41
Undé Ki Sabji, 30/31
Urud Ki Sukhi Dal, 114/115
Vegetables: Biryani, 214/216
    Carrot and Peas - North
        Indian Style, 192/193
    Fried Bhindi or Okra, 157
    Mashed Aubergine - North
        Indian Style, 176/177
    Mixed Vegetable Korma, 112/113
    Onion and Spinach Pakora, 98/99
    Peas and Indian Cheese, 118/119
    Potatoes Boiled in their
        Jackets, 23
    Potato Curry, 198/199

Potato Paratha, 132/133
Potato Patties, 162/163
Pulao with Nuts, 94/95
Red Beans - North Indian -
    Punjabi Style, 200/201
Stuffed Green Peppers, 184/186
Stuffed Tomatar, 210/211
Vegetable Samosa, 44/47
Whole Cauliflower, 140/142
Vindaloo: Pork or Lamb, 80/81
White Split Urud Lentil, 114/115
Whole Cauliflower, 140/142
Whole Chicken with Nuts, Minced
    Lamb and Rice, 62/65
Whole Green Mung Beans - North
    Indian Style, 82/83
Yoghurt: Home made, 27
    Lassi, 68
    Tomato, Cucumber and
        Onion Rayta, 41